The Angels Beside Us

The Angels Beside Us

Winner of the 2020
Spiritual Writing Competition

GLYNIS AMY ALLEN

AUTHOR OF THE BESTSELLING *GHOSTS OF THE NHS*

A record of this publication is available from the British Library.

ISBN 978-1-910027-39-4

Typesetting by Wordzworth Ltd
www.wordzworth.com

Cover design by Titanium Design Ltd
www.titaniumdesign.co.uk

Cover image: S2-106 'Snow Angel' nebula,
by kind permission of the NASA

Published by Local Legend
www.local-legend.co.uk

To my wonderful husband Frank and to my family.

Acknowledgements

I am grateful to my publisher Nigel Peace,
who has given me the confidence and guidance to write this book,
and to Chrissie Astell for her support.

Disclaimer

All the personal names of individuals referred to in this book,
save those of the author's family, have been changed
to preserve their privacy.

PREVIOUS PUBLICATIONS

GHOSTS OF THE NHS

ISBN 978-1-910027-34-9

www.local-legend.co.uk

About the Author

Glynis Allen has been blessed with wonderful spiritual gifts, especially clairvoyance, passed down to her by her Grandma Mac, the local Wise Woman. She taught her granddaughter to speak with spirits and angels, especially when she needed help, and these abilities developed over the years through many extraordinary experiences. "It has been natural and a privilege," she says, "for me to carry on my grandma's legacy."

Glynis worked as a senior hospital nurse in the National Health Service for thirty years, mostly in Accident & Emergency wards. In her debut book, she gave us true accounts of the ghosts and spirits she encountered, such as seeing the soul peacefully leaving the body of the deceased and working alongside spirit doctors. Now she tells of her frequent encounters with beautiful and compassionate angelic beings who visited the sick to bring reassurance and healing.

Throughout her career, both as a nurse and then as a working medium, Glynis has studied these higher spiritual beings closely, learning their names and purposes. Alongside her revealing stories, she describes how each one of us can grow closer to our own guardian angels to receive their guidance in our spiritual lives.

It is unique and refreshing to have an account of mediumship and communication with the spirit worlds that is given in such a humble and down-to-earth way. This is a remarkable book, its stories as entertaining as they are evidential, and it is the thoroughly deserved winner of our national Spiritual Writing Competition.

Glynis Allen's website is *www.glynisallenpsychic.com*

Contents

Foreword
by Chrissie Astell

In these times of increasing uncertainty, we all search for guidance or reassurance of some kind. More and more people around the world are awakening to their own personal spiritual impulse, a heightening sensitivity, and for some that means a deepening of the connection between humanity and the angelic realms. All my life I've been aware of a powerful presence that I can only ever describe as 'Divine' – a deep personal sense of knowing that there was 'someone' listening to my prayers. How do I know this? Because I have been blessed by answers, happenings and the most beautiful angelic visitations.

But Glynis Allen has been blessed with one of the greatest gifts of all, she has clear sight, 'clairvoyance', and has been sensing and seeing the presence of angelic beings for decades. Glynis hasn't had just the odd vision, she has seen angels working alongside her time after time, in fact throughout her entire nursing career. And with great generosity of spirit she has shared her awareness and her gifts with others. Whether at times of transition, as loved ones were leaving this life and crossing the bridge to the next, or whether in situations of warning and guidance, angels have made themselves visible through her open, loving heart.

I look back at my own brief nursing career and wish that I had known Glynis then! To have worked alongside someone with such spiritual gifts would have saved many years of wondering. These stories, explanations and deeply understood experiences are shared with such loving authenticity, bridging the gap between psychic phenomena and Divine presence.

What exactly are 'angels'? What is their purpose and are they accessible to everyone? These beneficent beings are integral to creation itself, ineffable, elusive and almost beyond comprehension. I know them as spiritual beings of Divine Light, with high vibrational frequencies resonating with the power of pure love. When we accept this, we can resonate with love too and in this way open our hearts to the angels' call.

Chrissie Astell, Spiritual Facilitator and Educator, and Healer

Chrissie is the author of *Discovering Angels*, *Gifts from Angels*, the *Guardian Angel Oracle* card set and *Seven Steps into Angel Light* (Watkins Publishing).

Her website is *www.AngelLight.co.uk*

1

Guardian Angels

The Red Emergency Phone rang. Two young boys swimming in a river had got caught in the reeds below and were drowning until a passing man had managed to free them both. He then simply walked away.

What a strange thing to happen, I thought, because that place was isolated and not many people knew about the river there. The kids were about eleven years-old and in shock, but they wanted to tell me their story. It was a secret place they'd found while playing in the woods and they'd never seen anyone else in the area.

The eldest said, "We had a bet who could dive in the deepest. The water was murky but we were having a good time so we both dived in. There were long reeds under the surface and Andy got caught up in them. I tried to loosen his legs but I couldn't and I was scared we were both going to drown. Then suddenly the reeds lit up like a bright torch shining through them and then it felt like someone was pulling us up into the air, both at the same time. We just lay on the riverbank exhausted and not knowing what happened." I asked him how his parents had managed to find them there.

"My Mam says she heard a voice that said, 'Your boy is in danger' and then, 'Wild wood', so she got some neighbours to do a search and they found us." I told him they were very lucky to be alive and asked whether the man had said anything to them, but no, he'd just walked away.

"He was a bit funny-looking, though," said the other lad. "He had a face like a nice-looking woman and really golden hair." I asked what he was wearing. "It was a like a white woman's blouse," he told me, "but he had trousers on like the ones Asians wear – we've seen pictures of people like him at school." He then said something very surprising. "I think he must have been picking flowers because he had them in his hand, they looked like white bluebells. You know, I remember now, as he walked away he waved and said, 'Peace be with you, boys.'"

I said nothing at the time but I believe it was an angel that rescued the boys – and the one associated with both children and water is the Archangel Gabriel, known to watch over children and guide them when they reach a perilous path. His name means God's Strength and he has always been shown in paintings carrying white lilies. Of course, no-one knows for sure which angels appear in our lives and for what reasons, but I have spoken to many people who believe they have been visited by an angel and they are usually identifiable by their appearance. Sometimes, though – as in this case – an angel does not have wings or a halo but comes in human form. Here he had golden hair, wore a white top and trousers and was carrying flowers.

This story has a rather wonderful sequel. Many years later when I was working in another area, I came across one of those boys who was a grown man by then with a family. He told me that the reeds had been so tangled around both his legs there was no way anyone could have freed them and save his life. With tears in his eyes he said, "Every day I pray to that angel with thanks for saving my life."

I was shocked. "You think it was an angel who saved you?" I asked.

"A few weeks later," he said, "I had a dream and that man who we thought was a woman came into my dream and said, 'You were saved by an angel.' I had to tell you because I think you knew all along. When we said about how the man looked, I could see in your face that you believed us and thought it was an angel." I smiled and nodded. "I knew it!" he went on. "I'm glad I found you. We did come back with some flowers and chocolates for you but you weren't there."

Then he opened his coat and pulled up his jumper to show me an amazing tattoo of coloured angel wings on his chest, and I now saw that he was wearing the white collar of a priest. "That day changed my life," he said, "and I now work for God." How profound and amazing, I thought, that he was saved by an angel and now acknowledges this in his work, spreading love and light to the world.

Another child I will never forget was a young girl who had advanced lung cancer. I was asked to sit with her, her tiny hand slipped into mine. She would often turn to the wall, smile and ask questions like, "Am I going to die tonight?" When I asked her why she did that she told me there were faces of angels on the wall; when she talked to them, they answered and 'told the truth'. Then she said, "Don't move, there's an angel behind you and looking at me."

I wanted to turn around of course but she squeezed my hand to stop me. I could feel a presence, though, and I could smell white roses. The girl's face was such a beautiful picture of radiance that I couldn't help myself – and as I turned around I could not believe what I was seeing. The figure was very tall, with white hair and unforgettable pale blue eyes.

The girl said, "I know why she is here, nurse. I was praying this morning with the priest and we said a prayer for my soul." Then she turned back to talk intensely to the wall again about what she was going to do when she got to Heaven. I told her I was just going to fetch her medication but she said she didn't want any, she wanted me to stay with her and hold her hand because she was ready to go with the angels to see her Mum and little girl.

"Did you see that angel's eyes?" she said, her voice now becoming very low. "Sky blue, they were my daughter's eyes looking at me. Nurse, would you put me in that pink nightdress with the teddy bears on it? My daughter will know it's me then."

A lump formed in my throat. She was actually planning what to wear when she died. Her cold hand started to tingle, she closed her eyes and went into a deep sleep; I stayed with her holding her hand as her soul slowly lifted up. She was on her way to see her daughter.

Another nurse came to help me do the last offices for this beautiful girl and we worked silently, there was no need for words because she had passed over with dignity and love. As we wrapped her, we both heard a 'whoosh' and I smelled the fragrance of white roses again, the gentle fragrance of the angels taking her home.

I had a nursing career of thirty years and worked in many different healthcare settings gaining a vast experience of different specialities. In that time I came to know that there are so many angels out there who want to help us in any way they can, whether it be at times of danger or to support us in grief. As a spiritual medium, too, I have been able to connect with the spirits of the deceased and been privileged to have seen angels in many different guises.

This has been a familiar path for me since childhood, brought up listening to angel stories that my Grandma Mac used to tell me. She was a staunch Catholic but also the local Wise Woman, and people would come to see her with all sorts of problems that she treated with herbs and potions. I helped her mix the ingredients and still carry on her legacy today.

Every Friday we would make little fairy cakes and ginger beer for Father Regan who would come to collect his half-crown for the church funds. We would sit and talk about angels and the Bible – and my favourite heroine, Joan of Arc. The story says that she was visited by Archangel Michael when she was eleven years old and told she must save France. I loved to listen to Father Regan's Irish twang as he reminisced about his life in Ireland, how he became a priest, and told stories about the many heroic feats of saints.

One that stayed with me was about Saint Bernadette of Lourdes, canonised in 1933, because my auntie had travelled to Lourdes for healing. It also fascinated me because Saint Bernadette had seen visions of the Virgin Mary, whom my mother had been named after; she witnessed seventeen apparitions but no-one believed her. The story goes that Virgin Mary advised her to drink from the spring that flowed in the rock grotto, but there was no spring, so Bernadette dug with her bare hands for three days until the water sprang up. This water is now renowned worldwide for providing miracle cures.

We rarely went to church because Grandma's legs were bad so we made a point at two o'clock every afternoon of praying to a different angel in her bedroom. She knew all the angels' names and which special jobs they had, each one with a speciality because of their spiritual nature. When Uncle Alan took her out in his car, she would always ask Archangel Michael to protect them from harm (Uncle Alan was a good driver but she just felt better asking for his protection!). When she became ill, it was always Archangel Raphael she asked for healing.

Grandma Mac had always been a worker. Whenever I stepped into her house there was either washing, baking or sewing going on. She was a very clean and honest lady with the whitest net curtains on the street. She also had a strong gift of clairvoyance but sadly was forbidden to use it because of the family's Catholic faith.

My much-loved Grandma Mac and Uncle Alan are no longer with us but I feel blessed that she left me with a spiritual gift and that now I am the storyteller. We all have a guardian angel who is our protector and gives guidance. My Grandma Mac also guides me; I feel her with me and she always brings the fragrance of Blue Grass perfume.

When I was twenty-one years old I found that I was going to have my first baby. At that time I lived a long way from Grandma and my Mam and visited them twice a week, on a Monday and Thursday. I would smell the baking as soon as I went in. This day, Grandma said her legs were very bad so would I clean the stairs for her? I thought, 'Well, I'm pregnant – shall I tell them?' but a voice in my head told me not to. Grandma Mac smiled slowly at me and I thought, 'She knows I'm pregnant so why isn't she saying anything?'

I made the tea while she lit up a cigarette, sitting in the green rocking chair that no-one else was allowed to sit in. I was in a chair facing her and then saw a sort of silver halo appear around her head; she saw me looking at it and asked what was wrong, but I said nothing because it made me feel uneasy. I was then more uncomfortable because I never lied to Grandma.

There was a knock at the door and she went to answer it, leaving me to watch her rocking chair begin to move on its own as an angel wearing a lilac robe appeared beside it. Well, now I had to tell Grandma what I'd seen when she came back in.

"Yes, they have come to comfort me and pave my way to Heaven," she said. "I have cancer and there's no treatment." Then she turned to look straight at me. "Now you know why I want you to always use your gift." I didn't ask any questions, I felt too devastated that she was not going to see my baby. How can life be so cruel?

Later, I cried myself to sleep but then felt something touch my face. I opened my eyes to see the same silver halo I had seen over Grandma's head only this time it had a face inside it, a sweet-looking cherubic face. I thought, 'I have to tell her about the baby as soon as possible' so I did on my next visit. She just smiled and said, "I know. And I've hung on 'til you were having a baby so I can go in peace."

The following day I had an awful feeling that time was running out for her and a voice in my head said, "It's the last time you'll see her." By now I was used to getting these messages; Grandma had once told me that it was my spirit guide. This time when I opened the door it wasn't baking I could smell but frankincense. Father Regan was giving Grandma the Last Rites, a final purification of one's soul and a preparation for entering Heaven. Even after all these years, my Grandma Mac is still guiding me. If I have a problem, I ask her advice and she gives it by showing me scenes in my mind or by sending me a sign.

When it came to the day of her funeral, I had been having terrible morning sickness so I overslept. I had to catch two buses and when I got to the church it was empty, I had missed her funeral. I was very upset as I went to the graveyard – Protestant on one side, Catholic the other side, with over three hundred graves – and it was very foggy and scary with no-one about to ask where her grave was. I closed my eyes and asked for guidance from the angels to help me find Grandma, then wandered around until suddenly the fog cleared and there it was. Later as I walked away with a heavy heart, I clearly heard her say, "I love you, no matter what."

My mother lived next door to Grandma's and it was soon clear she couldn't cope without her own Mam, quickly going into a decline. My daughter was born, her first grandchild, with the same colour eyes as my Grandma. Time passed and I had my son, nearly losing my life giving birth to him, but Grandma came to reassure me that everything would be okay.[1]

Grandma Mac would have been so proud to see me in a nurse's uniform. And starting my training did not stop Spirit from showing

---

[1] This and other stories of my early days are told in my book *Ghosts of the NHS* (Local Legend, 978-1-910027-34-9).

me visions and whispering in my mind. At times I thought I would go crazy with all the hard work and studying with two small children to look after; I was tired out but I was determined to do the training and one day be a healthcare teacher – big ideas for someone who left school with no qualifications and worked in a mill because I had to bring up my sisters while Mam was having a breakdown. We were struggling but she had to undergo those awful electric shock treatments, so we were happy to do what we could. When she came home she was a different woman, happy for a while and that was good to see until finally she was diagnosed with lung cancer. My sisters looked after her at home.

On the eve of my birthday I was sitting with Mam when I noticed a pink aura over her head. She whispered, "My Mam's here, she has come for me." She had prayed daily for Grandma Mac to come for her and be reunited in the spirit world. Then I heard the words "Silver pin" spoken very softly. Recently, I had been writing about the Goddess Artemis whose colour is silver. Knowing that Mam was near the end of her life, I went into another bedroom for a few moments alone to say a prayer and ask the angels to care for her when I saw a silver pin on the carpet… yet Mam had never sewn or used pins and this bedroom was not used by anyone. When I went back to the other room, the book I had been reading was open at a description of Archangel Anael, who brings comfort, healing and support during bereavement. Tellingly, Archangel Anael wears a silver pin.

As I sat reading to Mam, I felt a shimmering presence and Mam said, "They are here. The angels… they must have heard you reading to me about them and the way they help us." She took my hand and said, "I always loved you even though I didn't show it. Can I borrow Grandma's rosary beads? I am going with the angels soon and I just want to say a prayer." I gave her my treasured rosary beads with a feeling that I wouldn't see Mam or the beads again.

She passed away the following day, my birthday. That night I dreamed about her as a young woman, with me as a child and how happy we'd been when we went pea picking with her friend. She said to me in the dream, "I passed away on your birthday not to remember my death but to remember the mother-and-daughter bond we once had." I never did get my rosary beads back, they were lost when the flat was cleared out, but I do still have the silver pin stored away with little gifts that Mam bought me,

Grandma had five boys and one girl, my mother, and all left home and married except my Uncle Alan. He worked at the pit and looked after the pit ponies; I would take him his sandwiches at dinnertime and sit with the donkeys while Alan fed them. He was a happy soul who loved his horse racing and would often say to me, "If you can get to the bookie's in five minutes, put this bet on. If it wins I'll give you two bob." I'd fly like the wind to place his bets though he wasn't too forward in giving me my two bob. I wondered how he would cope when Grandma died; well, he met and married a woman then divorced in three months, too set in his ways.

One afternoon he came into my mind and I had a bad feeling about him; I could also feel my Grandma Mac close by and smell her Blue Grass perfume, so I knew something was wrong. I phoned to ask if he was okay and he confessed that he was losing blood when he peed, so I knew he was in trouble because Grandma didn't send a sign for nothing. It had been going on for months and he had not gone to the doctor's because "It's private." He only saw a doctor when I made the appointment for him, then was admitted to hospital with prostate cancer. It had spread throughout his body and there was no hope for him.

I went to visit him in hospital and as I walked into the cubicle I clearly saw an angel's face looking down; it had dark red-brown hair, dark eyes and was wearing a light blue robe. I knew then his time was running out. Alan smiled and said, "I saw an angel, it touched my hand." In my mind I heard Grandma say, "He needs a priest", so I told Alan I'd ask a priest to come and chat with him.

The following day when I walked into the cubicle there were two different scents, one of death and the other of the baby talcum powder I always associate with visiting angels, so I knew his time was near. He held my hand and said, "I saw that angel again last night" then I heard a loud 'whoosh' and glimpsed something that looked like large yellow wings that enfolded Alan. He passed away a few minutes later.

It was an especially difficult time because my husband's cousin was also deteriorating badly with congestive cardiac failure; he was in his eighties and a very difficult man, had no time for women and never married so lived with his Mam and Dad until they died. We were the ones who then looked after him. He was argumentative, dogmatic and challenging though also quirky and funny at times. I noticed he was becoming forgetful, snappier than usual and breathless. One day we called to take him shopping, finding the door open and he was on the floor. "I am not going to hospital," he said, but I called an ambulance and went with him.

I visited him next day and he looked very poorly. He said, "I am scared of dying, will you stay with me?" which I thought took a lot of courage for him to say. He asked me what happens when we die and I told him about my beliefs, probably the longest conversation he'd ever had with me. I stayed with him throughout the night as he slipped into a coma and his breathing changed. Then at the back of his bed a shimmering pink light developed into a face and a soft voice said, "We are ready to take you home." A mist appeared and from that rising mist I saw his soul leave his body with an angel at his side.

He had asked me to put lilies on his coffin so I did that and took photos of them for relatives who could not attend his funeral. Later, I deleted the picture. When I myself needed an operation in hospital, I received a text on my phone from my husband – the photo of those lilies! No-one else had taken this photo and I had deleted it… "Why are you sending me funeral flowers?" I demanded, rather cross. He assured me that he hadn't sent it. Well, even though he had no idea about modern technology, I think I know who it was, saying 'Thank you.'

There was one more family bereavement in those early years. My mother-in-law Flora was an amazing lady, like a mother to me and nothing was ever too much trouble for her. I worked with her on the family market stall until I became pregnant when she said, "I don't want you taking any risks with my first grandchild – you're sacked!" Flora later developed kidney failure and then had a thyroid operation that wasn't successful, so she retired to look after the kids while I got a job (ironically, beginning my nursing career).

At New Year, I put my arms around her shoulders as we watched the fireworks knowing that she was becoming weaker and we would lose her very soon. Suddenly, she pointed to a bright white light in front of us and we both saw a beautiful Being in a long white gown, which somehow I knew was Archangel Gabriel. Flora said, "She is coming for me." When we went back into her flat, the fragrance of white roses was really strong. Flora died soon after this.

The wake was held at a local hotel, a small gathering with music playing softly in the background. Just as everyone sat down and I raised a toast, saying, "We love you so much, Flora", all the lights in the hotel went out! When the electricity came back on, the next song playing was Angels. So I knew that Flora was there with us and telling us that she was with the angels. We left the hotel not with sadness but happy that Flora had come through – and she wasn't finished yet. When I got home, I found that some Sympathy cards had been knocked over and were scattered on the floor; all the ones facing upwards were the ones with pictures of angels on the front. I knew that Flora was doing just fine.

Along with these difficult family experiences, I've had my own personal angelic encounters when I was in great need. Some three decades later, I would lose my job due to an accident and health issues, which made me deeply upset, and I was often in excruciating pain.

One cold November day, I stayed in bed because I couldn't move. There was only my husband Frank and I in the house along with our two dogs, Mollie and Paddy, who would lie on the bed beside me knowing how poorly I was. When Frank brought me tea and biscuits we shared them! I was taking very strong pain relief medication but it didn't shift the pain, and eventually I fell asleep.

I dreamed I was living in Heaven, with beautiful people all around me who looked slim with lovely long blonde hair, both male and female. One of them walked towards me carrying a silver cup for me to drink out of. He was wearing a green gown, his feet were bare and I noticed he had brown eyes that looked strange and reminded me of the crystal Tiger's Eye. I sat down on a rock that was soft and warm and began to feel very peaceful. There were other people dancing nearby and I saw swirling lights around them like flashing coloured electric light bulbs. The man said, "You will be well. Pray to me, Raphael is my name."

I woke up to find Mollie licking my tears. I was wary of moving and sitting up but something felt different and I found that I could sit up without too much pain, then get out of bed without the stick I had been using. It was the first time in two weeks that I was able to get up for a few hours. To this day, I believe that I received angelic healing.

During those dark days, I also had a brain haemorrhage that left me with a left-sided weakness and partially deaf, and I was to have surgery to restore my hearing. The night before my operation I was in a ward with four very elderly women awaiting surgery; I couldn't sleep so I was reading a book. At about 3 a.m. I heard very low, soft singing and looked up to see one of the old ladies nearby 'playing the piano', her fingers plucking at the bedsheets. There was also someone standing beside her in a white dress, and I assumed it was one of the nurses come to ask her to be quiet.

The figure turned to face me. She had sapphire blue eyes and wore a golden belt around her waist. I got out of bed and was going over to the lady when I saw a mist rising above her body as the figure then vanished. In my own nursing career I had seen this many times and I knew what had happened – the lady's soul had left her body before my eyes.

I went to fetch the night nurse and told her that the old lady across from me had died, but she replied, "Don't be daft, I was with her fifteen minutes ago, she can't have." She came over and touched the lady's hand then ran off to ring the trauma team. I did think that was rather pointless since the woman had died and should not have to go through the ritual and indignity of CPR, but then doctors and nurses always do try to revive patients. Fortunately in this case, the Registrar checked to see whether the lady had a signed DNR form (Do Not Resuscitate), which she did.

Next day, I was taken to theatre for my operation – without anaesthetic because of the brain haemorrhage! – and I prayed to the angels for help and healing. The following morning, I felt strong and confident. Unfortunately, the operation was unsuccessful but I was just happy that the angel of death had not come calling for me too.

2

The Early Years

When I took the entrance exam for Nursing, I qualified to train as a Registered General Nurse (RGN) for three years but I opted for the State Enrolled Nurse (SEN) training for two years. I told the Head of Nursing who interviewed me that I had two children to look after at home so two years would be long enough. She replied, "You will regret it!"

SENs get all the menial jobs whilst the RGNs are involved with medical care. Yet I never did regret my choice because I loved the role of being a 'bedside nurse'. It sounds cosy doesn't it? Well, not exactly – it includes a lot of bedpan washing, cleaning of sluices and dealing with patients' false teeth. But I helped to care for many wonderful people, had extraordinary experiences and made lifelong friends with some amazing nurses.

My first year was as an auxiliary nurse (now known as healthcare assistants) working on a chest unit where a lot of patients had lung cancer. I soon began to realise that I was being spiritually guided every day, although it took some getting used to. My psychic gifts are hereditary and at this point I'd never had any training in 'mediumship' or the like. But no, the voices I was hearing weren't signs of schizophrenia, they were spirit guides helping me. My visions weren't hallucinations. It wasn't diabetic retinopathy, the colours I clearly saw around people were their auras. I knew when patients came into the ward whether they would be going home again because it was written in their auras; I knew what condition they were suffering from and where it was affecting the body.

Over the years, in hospital and later while working as a medium and doing hundreds of readings, I have been able to recognise illness in someone when I see them. Sometimes it's a person's aura, sometimes a vision or a word from my guides; and in some cases, I know this has saved a life. As a young nurse back then, I didn't always know what to make of these things but I did know that if I told my colleagues they would think I was mad! So I learned to keep quiet until, gradually, I became more confident and knew what to say (or not).

In the early days of nursing, everyone makes mistakes and I still fondly recall my first mishap (although I have to say I wasn't the only one to have done this). However, even at these times I was blessed to receive angelic support.

I had been allocated to a ward for elderly men where the Sister was a real dragon, arrogant and rude, and she loved to show the young nurses up. Even the consultants were afraid of her and one of them whispered to me, "When she retires, we're going to throw the biggest party ever." She had a strict regime and, in particular, every patient had to have their false teeth soaked in mouthwash and all collected up in individual pots. We had to take these pots – twenty-five pairs of false teeth – to the sluice and clean each pair individually.

My great friend Vera, who never stopped talking, was in the same group as me then and we did practically every ward together. She had a wonderful warm heart but could easily, shall we say, get distracted. We were at the sluice with the teeth one day and Vera was chattering away, not concentrating. Suddenly she said, "Bugger this for a lark!" and tipped all the teeth jumbled up together into the sink. I gasped in horror and then it dawned on her what she had done.

When we had finally stopped laughing, I put my hands together and prayed to the angels, "Please get us out of this mess." Well, I didn't expect anything to happen because even then I understood that we should only ask for angelic guidance when it's really important, like a serious upset or a matter of life and death.

We scrubbed those teeth until they shone and placed all the patients' pots on the trolley in case Sister came past, so she would think we knew what we were doing. Then a soft pink glow filled the room and even Vera could see it. Could we be getting out of trouble after all with angelic help? We each took pairs of false teeth out of the sink one by one and laid them on the trolley, feeling as though we were being guided to put them in the right pots. Then we wheeled the trolley out, giving the patients a big smile as we fixed their teeth back for them. After lunch, Sister called us both over…

"I want a word with you two," she said, and we looked at each other guiltily. "I want to congratulate you both," she went on, "the patients are saying that their teeth have never felt so fresh. Well done, girls, you can both have a couple of hours off."

Once we were outside, Vera lit up her ciggie and let out a long sigh of relief. I said, "You owe me one now, it was me that got you out of trouble there." Well, I think we had some help from the Boss upstairs. We thought we'd got one over on Sister but no, there was a price to pay. She told us that we'd done so well with the false teeth that the job was ours until we left the ward.

Angles have the power to turn bad situations around in rather more important ways. The nursing training included a period in either Obstetrics or Gynaecology (Obs 'n Gynae) and I was pleased to be allocated to Obs because being on the gynaecological ward would have stirred up too many painful memories of when I'd been a patient there myself undergoing a hysterectomy to remove my cancer. The ward Sister here was nice. She told us to bring our own cups, some knitting or a book to read, because sometimes we'd be too busy to get a break, babies being so unpredictable. I soon felt lucky to have my two healthy children, a girl and a boy; there was one lady there who already had seven sons because she and her husband 'kept trying' for a daughter!

There was another student starting on the ward the same day as me. Alice was young, small and slim like a little mouse; she had no children but lived with her fiancé. One day we were waiting together for a meeting when she suddenly started to cry. "This is my worst nightmare," she confided, "babies being born and all that goes with it." I told her we would work together and I'd help her get through it, and as I put my arm around her I felt a kind of electric shock. A voice in my head said, "She's lost a child." Now I knew why she was so upset.

I was asked to help a mother bathe her new baby while Alice made the beds because she had no experience of motherhood; she looked relived. After this things were quiet so Sister said we could go to the library or do some shopping as long as we were back for the afternoon Baby Clinic. Being older, I decided to take Alice under my wing and try to help her – there was some sort of deep sadness in her – so I said, "Let's get a coffee and talk about what we want to learn from this allocation." When we were alone, she opened up.

"I hated it the minute I walked onto the ward," she said. "Terrible memories came flooding back and I'm sure Sister recognised me…" Alice had been thirteen years-old when she met an older man who, of course, said he loved her and that they'd get married when she was old enough. When she found out she was pregnant, he'd accused her of 'going with other men' and refused to accept any responsibility; then he'd moved away and cut all ties with her, leaving her on her own.

As she was telling me this, the room seemed to dim with a pale green light and I felt the presence of an angel in our midst bringing the fragrance of white roses. Alice noticed it too but I didn't say anything because she might have thought I was mad and, worst of all, she could tell other people and then I'd be labelled for the rest of my career.

Before Alice carried on with her story, she looked pleadingly at me with tears in her eyes and said, "No-one else knows about this, please don't tell anyone." I reassured her that we all make mistakes, these things happen and she was not to worry, her secret was safe with me. Her mother had said she could keep the baby and she would help to raise it but when she was seven months pregnant she had started to bleed. She had come to this very ward where we were now training and her baby boy had been stillborn. "I felt at the time that God was punishing me for having him," she sobbed. We carried on chatting about the stigma of these things and how people could be so judgemental back then, then as we stood up to leave the room turned a beautiful pink colour. Alice simply said, "I suppose they have this coloured lighting to help calm people down in here."

I knew different. And as I opened the door I heard a voice in my head say, "She is with child. The Lord giveth and the Lord taketh away." I looked at Alice and suddenly knew that she was having a baby girl but didn't yet know she was pregnant. Two weeks later, she came up to me beaming and said, "I have some-thing to tell you – but I think you already know. I'm having a baby. Last night I had a dream where an angel held my boy in his arms and said, 'He is coming back to you.' So I saw the doctor this morning and I'm three months gone. And another thing, my fiancé has just been offered a well-paid job down south, so I'm leaving soon."

I was thrilled for her and because I trusted her now I told her that, yes, angels do bring messages in our dreams. "And do you remember when the room went green?" I asked her. "That was a healing ray from Archangel Raphael, the master healer. The angels were sending you healing. And I'm sure the pink light we saw means you're having a little girl." She replied, "But why would the angel say 'he' is coming back?"

19

Well, Sister soon noticed that Alice looked blooming so the secret was out. She turned to me, too, and said, "I wondered why you seemed to be protecting her."

Alice was leaving at the end of the week and I still had a niggling feeling that there was 'something else', so I got out my pendulum and asked, "Is Alice having a girl?" The answer was 'Yes'. Then I asked, "Is Alice having a boy?" The answer was 'Yes' again. Mystery solved, she was having twins. My mother-in-law Flora was a brilliant knitter so I asked her to knit two baby coats and bootees, one set pink and one blue, and I gave them to Alice as a leaving present. "Do you know something I don't?" she asked. I shrugged and said I wanted to make sure she had one of each, just in case!

A year later, a letter arrived from Alice with a photograph of her and her twin babies, a boy and a girl, and I thought back to those words I had heard, "The Lord giveth and the Lord taketh away."

It's always heart-warming when other people see the angels' signs too and it's not just me, and I'm especially pleased when someone instinctively knows they can confide in me about their experiences. The Drunken Sailor was one example… When the Red Phone rang at 2 a.m. and the paramedic said, "We're bringing in a male aged around fifty, found unconscious on a bench in town, smells of alcohol", everyone groaned – it was Sailor again. We called him that because he was always drunk on rum (he told us that he'd got addicted to it when he was in the Navy) but whatever our personal thoughts were he was always treated with respect and received the same care as any other patient. He carried his belongings in a plastic bag, consisting of a few photos of his children and a bottle of rum. I felt so sorry for him having such a hard life – and where were his family?

When they brought him in he stank of dirt, had long hair and beard, wore a damp woolly hat and his clothes were sticking to him. I removed his hat and noticed a large gash at the back of his head; he had obviously been assaulted and he had cuts on his hands perhaps from protecting himself. I said to him, "You're safe now, in hospital. How did you get that big cut on your head?" He glared at me and said, "Bugger off!"

I started to take his vital signs and realised they were looking unstable and becoming dangerous so I shouted for the doctor. He came rushing in but then said, "Why are you calling for me? The man is obviously drunk so he can wait – I have poorly people to see to." Well, he was stressed but that was unforgivable. I calmly asked him to take a look at the ECG and put some gloves on to inspect the wound... We eventually got Sailor stabilised and I took him to x-ray.

By now he'd become very quiet, then he turned to me and said, "Nurse, I've seen an angel. It looked at me and smiled, after them youths left me for dead." He was kept on the medical ward for a few days of observation and kept telling everyone else that he'd seen an angel; naturally, most people were sniggering behind his back, calling him a stupid drunk. One day, I had to go to that ward to collect some equipment and Sailor saw me and called me over.

"Can I tell you something?" he began. "I really did see that angel. I know people think I was just drunk, but I saw it when them lads were kicking the shit out of me. They just stopped suddenly, like someone was protecting me." I believed him. "Something stopped them," I agreed, "otherwise things would have been much worse." (Actually, I phoned the police to report the assault, even though Sailor didn't want me to, because I felt he might receive some help if it was made official.)

Six months passed by. I was doing triage when a man came in with two teenage girls; one had fallen over skateboarding and had fractured her wrist. The man said, "You're the nurse that was kind to me, aren't you?" Well, I try to be kind to everyone but I didn't recognise this chap at all. "I'm the Drunken Sailor, nurse, as your doctor called me. Remember I had a gash to the head?" I smiled and nodded. "Well I really did see an angel that night," he went on, "and it saved my life in more ways than one. My family heard about the attack and came to see me – now I'm back with my wife and children and not drinking anymore. Yes, I can still see it now. He was dressed in blue with saffron-coloured hair."

I thought, 'I know who that is, it's Archangel Michael the Warrior' but I didn't say anything except, "I'm very happy for you. Now, let's get your lass a plaster on that wrist." But I couldn't hold back when I saw that same doctor from six months ago walking towards us. "Doctor, just a minute, guess who this is… It's our Sailor." They shook hands in good spirit and the doctor later confided in me: "You were right and I'm sorry, but I get so stressed when drunks come in and others need our help more."

I did feel some sympathy with that. Although every hospital doctor and nurse is dedicated to their work and genuinely cares for their patients, the life is often exhausting and can take its toll on personal relationships. Yes, even healthcare workers can be unkind to one another at times, without meaning to. When I was seconded to one particular A&E department, things were so busy and the teams already established that I myself felt left out, my skills ignored. On the other hand, support comes in unusual ways…

One day, feeling very low, I thought 'I am off to the library, then, do some research for my assignment.' Even there, the room was dark and dingy, horrible. I closed the door and started writing when all of sudden I felt a presence nearby and the room was no longer dark but filled with yellow rays (it wasn't sunshine because the weather outside was bad). This was, I realised, my angel looking out for me – Archangel Jophiel – and I heard a voice say, "Have faith." I felt a gentle embrace, too, as though wings were enfolding me and there was the familiar scent of baby talcum powder. After a few minutes there was a knock on the door.

"I've brought you a cup of tea, nurse," said the librarian. "I thought you looked quite down." Then she lifted her head and sniffed the air. "What's that perfume? It smells like baby powder – and the room looks very bright somehow. You seem to have a magic touch." Well, I could hardly tell her there was an archangel with us, could I? I thanked her for the tea and later went back to the A&E department.

"I'm so sorry you've been neglected," said the Charge Nurse. "It's just that we are so busy." I smiled and said, "It's fine, I went to the library." And this time, I was glad to have been ignored because I was able to have the most beautiful experience of a special angelic visit to lift my spirits.

During my training as a student nurse, I was already beginning to experience so many paranormal things alongside the busy workload that they almost began to seem, well, normal. We were allocated to each one of three hospitals in turn: one was for the elderly, another was for more acute cases with A&E attached, and the third included gynaecology and maternity wards, named East, South-West and Central. I loved the life of the hospital and the female orthopaedic ward I was allocated to, despite its heavy workload and other challenges; if you didn't have a bad back when you started, you would have by the time you left, and there was always a putrid smell of urine and faeces.

There were thirty patients, on traction, and nearly all elderly. 'Oh well,' I thought to myself, 'I am fit and ready to take whatever comes because I love my job.' A lot of the patients had what we now know as dementia (although we SEN nurses hadn't been taught about mental illness back then) and were either on traction for broken legs or were sitting in monstrous chairs that had a little food tray bolted to it; of course, the patients would often slide underneath their trays causing further injury. We would get the blame for that although no-one ever explained how we were supposed to keep an eye on all these patients while behind the privacy curtains seeing to other patients.

The hospital had been built in 1806 and there were long, dark corridors that were spooky to walk along especially at night. I had been on the ward for two weeks when it was my turn to do night duty. At 2 a.m. I had my meal – snacking wasn't allowed, we had to have a proper meal which felt very odd in the early hours – and I was just walking back to the ward when I saw a man wearing a large hat and dressed completely in black. He was carrying what looked like a staff with some sort of blade curled around it and had just come from my ward. Whoever was this and what was he doing in the hospital at two o'clock in the morning?

As he passed me, he said, "Goodnight, nurse." I could see that his face was unusually pale. Perhaps, I thought, he was one of the doctors taking a short cut through the wards to the doctors' mess where they were always having parties. When I got back to the ward I found it in chaos because not one but two patients had died, five minutes apart, which was very unusual. We were then so busy doing the last offices before the day staff came on duty that I forgot to mention the man in black to anyone else.

One of the patients who had died was a nun, in a private cubicle with candles burning all day and night near the bed at the request of her priest (imagine what Health and Safety would have to say about that these days). As I was washing her with a senior nurse, we both smelled a strong fragrance and I had a definite feeling that someone else was in the cubicle with us. All the lines had left the lady's face, her skin was smooth and beautiful and she looked serene as though all the cares of the world had left her.

Her rosary beads were in her hands so I gently removed them and put them on the bedside table, and the atmosphere turned a lovely soft pink with a very peaceful feeling. In those days, after the last offices, it was a nursing ritual to say a prayer and open a window for the soul to fly away (obviously, the soul doesn't need an open window to ascend) and to place a flower in the person's hands (yes, flowers were allowed back then too). As we wrapped this lady in a sheet, I placed a pink rose in her hands and we both clearly heard a voice say, "My beads." She wanted her rosary beads in her hands!

I turned to get the beads but they were gone, and my colleague couldn't have picked them up because she was at the other side of the bed. We searched everywhere – black bags, yellow bags, laundry bags with no sign of the beads. Then I had a sudden thought and said to my colleague that we'd have to unwrap the lady; incredibly, the rosary beads were wrapped around her hands now.

My colleague, who was very experienced, said, "Oh my God, I have never seen anything like that in all my years of nursing. How did that happen?" I said it must have been divine intervention. "Well, perhaps it was," she replied. "This hospital is so spooky. Do you know, there is a ghost who wears a big black hat and carries a sickle. He always seems to be around when there are deaths and a lot of people have seen him. We call him the Grim Reaper." I was only a trainee nurse then and I didn't think it would be a good idea to say, "Oh yes, he said 'Goodnight, nurse' to me on the corridor earlier."

I didn't see him again at that hospital because I was moved to a different placement, but I saw him often later throughout my life. And I soon learned that every hospital has these unearthly visitors; all nurses know about the Grey Lady who haunts the wards, visiting patients just before they pass over.

One day I was ready to start back at work after a break and I had to see the Nursing Officer, Missy, a lovely lady with very kind eyes that noticed everything. She said there was going to be a dinner dance 'to give the girls a treat' but she didn't know what to wear and needed my advice because I "always look so classy". There I was, come to be interviewed, and Missy was showing me half a dozen dresses! She was short and very overweight so nothing fitted.

"I was slim like you when I was training to be a nurse," she told me, "but I was bullied. And I had lots of boyfriends but my mother would never allow me to take one home, so I never married. Well, I am married to my career." As she tried on another dress, she remarked casually that she'd heard rumours about a ghost – or was it an angel? – especially in the Chest Unit ward, and wondered if I had seen it. I had been getting a bit of a reputation for this.

"Yes, I have, many times," I replied, equally calmly. "In fact, she's in this room and standing behind you!" Missy's eyes were like saucers and she told me off for messing about, so I asked her if she could smell anything. "Yes, white lilies," she said, not daring to look round. "That's her," I said. But I was now worried why the Grey Lady would be in this room – did it mean that Missy was going to pass over? The Grey Lady just looked at me and then vanished.[2] Missy chose a beautiful blue silk dress and looked very attractive. I left the office and walked down the steps where the Grey Lady was standing at the bottom as though waiting for me. Then she just shook her head and vanished.

A couple of weeks later we were told that Missy would be taking compassionate leave because her mother had passed away very suddenly. When she did return she came to find me on the ward, looking peaky and having lost weight, and asked me whether the Grey Lady had come to warn her about her mother. I mumbled something about maybe she had lived in the room Missy used as an office, but she then said, clearly a bit shaken, "I've seen her again myself today…"

Next day she came onto the ward in tears, telling me that her sister had now also died. "I'm going to retire," she said. "I've done my bit for nursing and I don't think I can cope with seeing the Grey Lady again. It might be for me next time." Well, I am pleased to say that Missy had a long life and I heard on the grapevine that she did find someone to love her after all. She had been an amazing Nursing Officer and deserved to be happy.

It's part of a SEN's job, of course, to care for those coming to the last moments of their lives. Personally, I have always felt privileged to be at the bedside then and, if I could offer some comfort, that was good. Although many people seem to fear death and don't like to talk about it, it is very often a peaceful and uplifting experience – for me as well as for the patient.

---

[2]   I've learned that the Grey Lady used to live in a big house that she opened up for wounded soldiers, and it later became Oakwood Hall Hospital. Her name was Elizabeth Sinclair and she became a Red Cross nurse, often now appearing in that uniform and usually to patients who were about to die.

3

Orbs, Lights And Feathers

Angels do not always appear as we might have come to expect, given the many paintings made throughout history, with golden hair, halos and large wings. Sometimes they walk among us looking like anyone else. Often, I have come to realise, they appear as orbs of light or flashing colours, or they might give us 'signs' such as a white feather in an unexpected place.

I had been working in Accident and Emergency departments and wanted to learn more about different aspects of A&E nursing so I took a six-month course that took me to several A&E departments including a large city hospital that had the more serious injuries coming through the doors. One day I was in the 'walking wounded' department when a young homeless woman walked in with her hand bandaged. She told me that someone had stuck a knife in her hand and now it was leaking "some horrible smelly stuff."

Before I removed the bandages I took her temperature and pulse; both were very high and then she started to vomit and shiver. The wound was infected and by now she was high priority because the infection was so bad it could cause the girl to have an amputation. I had a bad feeling about her. She was admitted to a ward and I got her settled in. As I was leaving I looked back and noticed a pink shimmering orb above her head with the face of an old lady in it. She looked so frail lying there in bed and my heart went out to her, with a dreadful feeling that she would pass over very soon; she needed to be aware how poorly she was in case she wanted to contact her family.

She told me she had no family, she lived on the streets and the people there were her friends and family, but I heard a voice say, "She is lying." Then another orb joined the first one with a sweet, angelic cherub face in it. She started to deteriorate in front of my eyes so I called a doctor over and asked him to move her to a side ward near the nurse station because I feared she was going to have a cardiac arrest. Unfortunately I was right; they fought to save her but to no avail.

Later, I was doing the last offices for her and a healthcare assistant came to help me. Straight away she said, "What's that pink glow at the top of her head jumping about? How scary!" I told her about orbs and said I thought this one was a spirit connected to the girl who had come to escort her to Heaven. Of course, then I had to say that I read a lot about these things; I wasn't going to make it known that I'm psychic because then I would either be ignored, laughed at or inundated with requests to 'tell fortunes'.

Just as I escorted the girl's body to the coroner's van, two distressed women came rushing up and one said, "Can you help us? My daughter was brought in here, she'd been stabbed in the hand." As I walked slowly back to A&E later, I wondered why the girl said she had no family. When her mother was interviewed it turned out that the girl was a drug user and her mother had thrown her out onto the streets.

It had been a very sad day. But then as I collected my belongings to go home, I clearly heard a voice say, "Thank you." And the healthcare assistant nearby said, "Wait a minute, you've got a white feather on your shoulder." I smiled as I walked to my car knowing that the girl had acknowledged our efforts to help her.

Sometimes, really challenging situations turn out more happily. Another hospital I worked in was cold and spooky with long corridors closed off at night and you didn't see anyone until the next morning unless you had an admission during the night. I was on night duty in the children's ward, adjacent to A&E which was noisy, and many kids were awake and crying for their mums. The ward phone rang at 2 a.m. to tell us of the admission of a three year-old child who had fallen downstairs and had multiple bruises on her body as well as a broken leg.

Both parents came along with four other children, and it was obvious that the parents were drunk. But you always have to keep on open mind in these cases. The doctor proceeded to take the history and the parents said the girl was not a good sleeper and had climbed out of her cot. I saw from the doctor's face that he was angry but he just told the parents he would order some pain relief for the child. As he left he passed me a slip of paper that read, 'Phone the Social Services emergency abuse number'.

I wondered what I should do. This was a junior doctor, not the casualty doctor who would normally make such a decision, so I didn't immediately make that call. Then as I was giving the child her pain relief I felt that familiar 'whoosh' and saw a pink light beside me as a voice said, "This child is loved." That was enough for me. Well, anyone who has children, especially three year-olds, will know what a handful they are and this family had six kids altogether. So I found myself having a bit of an argument with the doctor! He said he thought she had been abused whilst I pointed out that if Social Services got involved then this child and the five other children would have been removed in the middle of the night to a foster home. He replied, "Well, you aren't a doctor." "No," I said, "but I am a mother."

I went back to the girl's cubicle where her Mum was sitting with her. She said, "Nurse, there have been coloured lights dancing along the bed. Have you put some kind of special lamp on her?" I knew straight away that these were coloured orbs and the child had been visited by an angel to protect her. When the

29

incident was investigated later, it turned out that the side bars of the cot were faulty and the little girl had seen her chance to have a wander around. These things happen sometimes and we shouldn't be too quick to place blame on others. The girl made a full recovery.

I recall another sad case – thankfully, very rare indeed – of a doctor not doing his job properly. One young woman, who had been placed in a children's home as soon as she was born, arrived at hospital bleeding profusely from her wounds having attempted suicide. I saw straight away that her aura was a murky brown with a couple of red patches in it, and she was obviously stressed, her jaw clenched and her eyes downcast, and I felt so sorry for her. I led her to a cubicle so we could look at her wounds but she would not look up when I spoke to her, just kept muttering under her breath. Her wrists needed stitching so I said I would clean things up then fetch a doctor.

"You're new here, aren't you?" she said. It was true, I was on secondment from my usual hospital. "I thought so," she went on. "They don't like me in here, I heard them say I was a pest." I tried to reassure her that all the staff treat patients with respect but she didn't believe me, so I changed the subject and asked her why she kept trying to kill herself. "You wouldn't understand," she murmured, and I was trying to reassure her when the doctor arrived.

"You here again, Christine – how many times is it now, twenty-four?" As we moved away, I suggested to him that the young woman obviously had a problem that needed resolving, but he simply looked down at me over his gold-rimmed glasses and said, "You're new here, aren't you? You'll soon learn what A&E is all about. This sort of patient keeps coming in with attempted suicide but they never actually mean to do it." He didn't realise that I was already an experienced A&E nurse.

He told me to give her some Lignocaine while he went to get the stitches and I pointed out that I was not allowed to give patients that, it has to be a doctor. How unprofessional this man was, obviously used to getting away with doing and saying what he liked. He made things worse, having stitched the wrists up, by saying, "As before, Christine, I am referring you to a psychiatrist so you will have to wait with this nurse. If you want to run off like you generally do, feel free." The woman rolled her eyes and said to me, "Do you believe me now?"

When we were alone, I got Christine to tell me her story. From the day she was born she was placed in a children's home without knowing who her parents were, then when she was older she'd been told to leave the only home she had ever known. She lived in a small bedsit with no friends and no-one to talk to. I began to notice how the patches in her aura were getting bigger and more pink, which was a good sign that she was calmer now, and then I could see a presence nearby, with blonde hair and wearing a brown spotted dress, looking quite young. Christine continued with her sad tale and then suddenly asked, "What's them coloured lights that keep going off and on? They look like fairy lights. And are you wearing a strong rose perfume?" No, I always wore lime, basil and mandarin perfume.

Later, I made her some tea and a sandwich and saw that the lady spirit was still with her. Yet I began to have a bad feeling about her and my feelings never let me down; as I turned away I heard a voice say, "Danger!" There had been a road traffic accident and four people were badly hurt so I had to go and help the other staff. I did ask the charge nurse if I could stay with Christine but was told, "No, she's a regular. She'll soon be running off."

Something was not right. Was the spirit her mother – she did look like her – and were the coloured lights the orbs of angels around her? Eventually, I was able to go and check on her and as soon as I opened the door there was the smell of blood: she had unpicked the stitches and was fitting. I rang the emergency bell and put her in the recovery position while the spirit lady watched and smiled. The doctors did everything they could but Christine had a cardiac arrest brought on by loss of blood and shock, and I watched her soul rise alongside the spirit woman and drift away.

I cleaned myself up and began to get Christine ready for the coroner with another nurse. When I touched her face I heard a whisper, "She is safe with me now." She did look peaceful now. The other nurse said, "Can you smell roses?"

We found out that Christine's mother had died in childbirth but she'd had brothers and sisters who were still alive. If only she had known, things might have been very different for her; maybe she would have been a mum herself and had a good life after all, but it wasn't to be.

The doctor did apologise later for being so rude but I kept wondering why he and others had not seen the signs that could have saved Christine's life. Many doctors have just not been trained to understand mental health problems, yet they are so common and can happen to anyone in an instant due to stress or a nervous breakdown. We saw patients who self-harmed or attempted suicide almost daily; we treated them, sent them home and then they were back again and again. Yes, doctors and nurses give their life and soul to medicine, working long hours for little or no thanks and are not offered counselling; saying that, any signs of weakness and they would be on their way to losing their jobs. We all just carried on.

In a strange way, I suppose I was 'lucky' to be able to see the signs of angelic support for my patients. Once I was asked to escort a man who was very poorly to the large city hospital. He had spinal and head injuries caused when sledging down a snowy hill with his two children. The hill was pretty steep and had hardened to thick, slippery ice in places. The children were at the bottom with their Mum waiting for Dad to come sailing down when... Bam! He'd crashed straight into a tree.

Some people tried to put him in a recovery position (which was the worst thing to do because with spinal injuries any wrong movement can cause paralysis, though I suppose they just wanted to help). But one sensible person checked the man's airway, breathing and circulation (the 'ABC' routine). He was unconscious so couldn't feel the pain of his broken leg. The man was in a coma and in a critical condition but well enough to be transported to the large teaching hospital, although I have to say that the paramedic and I did not think he would survive the journey. The 'Glasgow Score' is used to assess patients in a coma and correlates with the severity of a brain injury and the prognosis. He went into cardiac arrest just as we got to the hospital where staff were waiting for us – five minutes later he might have died in the back of the ambulance.

On the way back to my hospital, the paramedic said, "He was very lucky tonight, I thought he was a goner. A good job the blue lights were flashing or we wouldn't have got to the hospital in time." I said, "Put them back on, I haven't eaten all day!" I didn't, however, tell the paramedic that we'd had company in the ambulance. I was taking the man's vital signs when I felt a 'whoosh' and the ambulance filled with a lilac glow and there were coloured orbs at the top of the trolley. As our patient started to deteriorate, the presence grew stronger and I caught the pale purple colour of wings in the corner of my eye (I've since learned that this was Archangel Michael come to protect this man). When we got back to the hospital the ambulance was in disarray so I thought I may as well clear it up to be ready for the next casualty. As I worked, a white feather drifted to the floor; no, it could not have come out of a pillow.

Three months later, I was doing a dressing clinic when one of the nurses told me that someone was asking to see me. It was the sledge man, now in a wheelchair and wearing a spinal collar. He said, "I wanted to thank you and the paramedic for saving my life." I always get embarrassed by praise but this time it didn't seem to matter because I was elated he had pulled through and had come to thank me. I said, "You really scared us, you were very poorly." What he said next brought a lump to my throat.

"Yes, I know. And I know there was a presence there while we were in the ambulance." Then he looked into my eyes. "You knew too, didn't you?" I replied, "All in a day's work. Next time you go sledging, watch out for the trees!"

Many years later he came into A&E again, this time with his child who had broken her arm falling off a swing. I happened to be on plaster duty that day so I applied the plaster on the little girl's arm, beginning to feel like one of the family. He said, "You don't know how grateful my family is to you." He was walking with a stick now, his spinal collar gone.

Sometimes we have to deal with cultural as well as medical issues. One Boxing Day morning the Red Phone rang to tell us that the paramedics were bringing an Asian boy, about ten years-old, who had been knocked off his bike by a car. He was unconscious with a broken leg and the paramedics had kept his cycling helmet on until he could be stabilised. As we got the Resuscitation Room ready for his arrival there was a loud commotion outside. The boy was arriving – and so were thirty of his relatives, screaming and wailing. Fortunately, we had two fantastic Asian doctors on duty that day so they could confer with the crowd and tell them to go home.

When the trauma call goes out, many doctors from specialised units answer it immediately. At any given time we could have orthopaedic, surgical, medical and children's doctors as well as our own staff, just coming along to see if they can help. This just shows how well the NHS works.

The boy was small for his age (he had been born early and wasn't strong) and he pulled at my heartstrings; he was wearing new bike gloves and helmet matching his new bike, clearly a Christmas present. The investigations revealed that he had a fractured femur and a sub-arachnoid haemorrhage (a brain bleed). He was stabilised ready for theatre and then discharged to the critical care ward; but he wasn't responding to stimuli so needed one-to-one 'specialising', and that fell to me.

His Mum and Dad and four other children were in the cubicle when I got there and I had to explain that there wasn't enough room for all of them because I would be looking after their son and there all the time. Dad left, heartbroken, with the other kids whilst Mum stayed, muttering prayers and then crying and wailing. She didn't speak or understand English so I had to phone the Asian doctor again to come and speak to her, taking her to the relatives' room so I could do the observations.

When I went back into the cubicle it was really hot, but then it suddenly turned cold and I heard a rattle as a kaleidoscope of changing colours appeared all around his bed like coloured fairy lights. Just as extraordinary, the boy then opened his eyes and looked around the room. I fetched back his Mum and the doctor, who said quietly to me, "I thought he was dying. How amazing is that? Does he now have a chance of recovery or is it just a fluke?" The lad soon fell back into a coma and I began to have a bad feeling about the situation.

The extended family was becoming a nuisance, crying and wailing outside the ward. I do understand it's their culture, but it becomes a hindrance when they are upsetting the other kids and their parents. The doctor told them to go home yet still they kept coming, even from hundreds of miles away and at two o'clock in the morning, to pay their respects. We decided to allow them to see the boy two at a time but then go home, because we wanted to respect their ways. The masses of sweets and fruit they brought would have filled several supermarket trolleys, and this was all sent to the kitchens to be distributed to other patients (health and safety wasn't as strict then as it is now).

By 8 p.m. I had been with the little lad all day and there was no improvement in his condition, though he was stable. Each time I washed and turned him he felt like a rag doll. His Dad was here now and I suggested he go and get himself some food and a drink while I did the observations. At around 8.30 I was giving the boy's mouth a clean when I began to feel a presence beside me. Usually this doesn't bother me, it's familiar, but in this instance it did: I clearly saw an angel in white with a cherubic face and tiny wings that looked unformed, so I knew then that the little lad would pass over.

I called the doctor back. The lad's observations were slowing down as the doctor examined him so he turned to the parents and had to tell them that their son's condition had deteriorated and he was not going to get better. With their permission, I lifted the child out of bed and put him in his father's arms, where he passed away. All the while, I could see the angel staying with the child though of course only I could see it; and much as I would have loved to have said, "The angels have come for your son", culture and my profession forbade that. The father said to me, "Why has my son got a smile on his face?"

As with every culture there are rituals and customs to be carried out with respect. Unfortunately, this was a tragic accident that had to be referred to the coroner to determine the cause of death, although his mother and sisters were allowed to wash him and put him in a gown before leaving. Finally, I went home. At that time, I had a son of my own around this boy's age and I can't imagine what state I would be in if the same thing happened to him. But kids cannot be kept locked up to keep them safe; and even though the little lad had worn a protective helmet, it still didn't save him.

Nursing is especially hard when children have been involved in an accident.

Another extraordinary experience also involved an Asian couple, this time elderly, with very different beliefs about the end of life to those of most people. I was working on a ward for tuberculosis (TB) patients who would be there for weeks at a time; they were not segregated but we were careful with the crockery and cutlery, each one having their own and kept away from other patients. (The World Health Organisation, WHO, estimates that 1.8 billion people have been affected by TB and 1.5 million of these have died.)

It was a friendly place and the consultant was a lovely man. At Christmas he would buy everyone a present, Guinness for the men and BabyCham for the women, and the patients usually gave him a present in return; one year he had twenty-three pairs of socks. One Christmas Eve we were doing a ward round to see how many could go home for Christmas Day (only two out of thirty patients were fit enough) when the phone rang telling us we needed to admit a couple who had just arrived from India.

They were both in their eighties and were very poorly, suffering from TB, and looked almost skeletal. My first thought was that they wouldn't be going home. The man explained that they had become stranded in India in a place where no-one spoke English and they'd had to live in a rat-infested hotel until they could contact someone to help them. The local policeman would even come to eat at the hotel every day with his seven children and they all had to share the same cups; that's probably how they had caught TB. Despite everything, the couple were devoted to one another and always held hands, which gave me a lump in my throat because it was looking grim for both of them. They were coughing up blood and sweating so much their beds needed to be changed three times a day. They shared a cubicle at the end of the ward where there were another six patients suffering TB; we didn't isolate these patients, not wanting to offend them, and they all sat around the same table to eat and converse with each other.

The old lady had to have an x-ray in another, larger hospital nearby and her husband insisted on going with her but I had to explain that the vehicle didn't have room. His mobility was compromised and he'd need a wheelchair. I told him that a nurse would be with his wife the whole time but he only became more agitated. "If I don't go with her she'll die," he said. But then, "I don't feel well, nurse, take me back to my bed. I want to die first because I can't live without her." Immediately, he had a respiratory arrest and although the doctors came flying from the other hospital and tried for an hour to save him they were unsuccessful.

"I knew he would die today," his wife said calmly. She didn't shed a tear. "My heart is broken but I will soon be joining him." I asked her how she had known that, thinking to myself that I hadn't seen any signs of impending death. She replied, "I dreamed that an angel was watching over us. It was Archangel Azrael, the angel of death." I asked her how she knew about angels and their names and she told me that they had been travelling around the world, visiting many sacred sites and even meeting the Dalai Lama.

When we did the last offices, the man's face looked very youthful and it felt peaceful in the cubicle. Then the other nurse and I both smelled a wonderful fragrance like roses and at the foot of the bed we saw shimmering coloured lights. A pale lilac orb had the elderly man's face within it and it looked like tears were forming there. Even I was flabbergasted now, as another fragrance came that I can only describe as sage and lemon.

Now, the consultant wasn't happy about the cause of death so he ordered a post-mortem and even I had a feeling there was something amiss here. That night I had a dream in which I was shown a red bag belonging to the lady, which she carried everywhere she went; at the bottom of it I saw a plastic bottle containing little pink tablets. Next day, I asked the lady as casually as possible whether she had any pills in her bag that we ought to know about; of course, she accused me of snooping in her bag although I would never have had a chance. Finally she pulled out the plastic bottle containing little pink tablets and said they were 'for her skin'... but I recognised them as morphine tablets, a controlled drug that she couldn't be allowed to keep. She started to cry and confessed that her husband had got them illegally and that's why he'd wanted to go with her for her x-ray. "God works in mysterious ways, doesn't He?" she said.

The following day I saw the lady at the end of the corridor, with a blue light beside her as she walked towards me looking luminous. I felt a shudder, knowing that she would be joining her husband soon. It wasn't long before I heard her shout to me that she was going to collapse, she was sweating and cold. As we got to her cubicle, we saw two white feathers on her bed. She simply nodded and said, "My husband sent those. He is coming for me." I knew she was right because I could smell the scent of white lilies. The trauma team did their best but her body was closing down now.

I asked if she would like a cup of warm milk and she replied, "Don't be silly, nurse, I am off to find my husband. You saw those white feathers he left to let me know he is coming for me." The fragrance was very strong now so I simply asked if there was anything else she needed. "Yes, I have a confession to make," she said. "My husband took those pills on purpose." I sat and held the old lady's hand until she peacefully passed away.

I packed up her belongings thinking that the couple had no relatives – there'd been no visitors – but then one day a priest came to collect their possessions. He said, "I was his brother. But after I became a priest he disowned me." At that moment, a white feather fluttered down to the floor, I've no idea from where. He said. "There you go, he's listening up there with the angels and his wife by his side."

4

Let's Talk About Death

We don't really like to talk about the end of life, do we? Yet it will come to us all and, whatever our beliefs, it would be good to be prepared. Perhaps I can help to take some of the mystery and fear away because I have witnessed so many deaths throughout my nursing career. And to watch the process begin and end is truly amazing. My Mam used to say to me, "Memories last longer than dreams" because they stay with us all our lives; and most of my memories on this subject are genuinely uplifting.

Yes, it's sadly true that some people pass over alone, or through traumatic circumstances and never have the chance to say goodbye, or don't realise that their friends and family were there for them and surrounding them with love. I still believe, though, that the soul knows what is happening on Earth and that they are not forgotten. Only recently I attended the funeral of an elderly neighbour who was a much-loved lady; the whole occasion was really sombre but I could clearly see the lady herself hovering nearby, inspecting the flowers and messages. I smiled to myself because it was just the sort of thing she would do.

I also know for certain that angels and spirits from the Other Side are there to meet the soul and guide them on their way. Sitting with someone and watching while they pass to the spirit world is the greatest privilege of my life and very moving. The veil between life and death is so thin and it always amazed me that I could see the soul rise above their shell of a body and just lift up and away (if you listen carefully, you might hear the silver cord make a cracking noise as it separates).

As mentioned in the last chapter, I spent some time on an isolated and peaceful ward for tuberculosis patients many of whom were terminally ill. We had a lot of Asian patients because unfortunately TB was rife in their community at the time. Adnan was a man of some importance and he would have many people visiting him, bringing him food that was delivered in flasks because he never ate hospital food. He told me, "When I was in Pakistan, I had a personal food taster." I laughed and said, "Well, there are plenty of nurses here who will taste your food for you!"

He was a very courteous man who always appreciated our work. One day he asked if we would do a favour for him and allow people to come and pay their respects to him the next Sunday. I was astonished that a patient would ask permission like this but some of the more experienced nurses laughed and said, "Just wait 'til they arrive!" Sunday afternoon was very quiet but then we saw a bus coming down the drive and at least twenty Asians got out. Adnan was only in a small cubicle so we had to push his bed outside onto the veranda. Lesson learned. Still, they left us lots of sweets, biscuits, chocolates, curry – and money.

Even though Adnan's condition appeared to be getting better, there was just some underlying feeling I couldn't shake off and I felt helpless. He stayed in bed most of the time and his wife and two sons came to wash and dress him every day so he was rarely left on his own. He was in a private cubicle and would get out of bed a few times each day to say his prayers; we had a doctor who did the same at particular times of the day so we were used to that.

One very hot day I asked him if he would like to sit outside but he replied that he wasn't feeling well, his chest was "on fire", so I took his temperature and blood pressure. They were normal, he wasn't sweating and he did not look ill, yet I felt that something was wrong and informed the doctor who arranged for another chest x-ray since it was three weeks since he'd had one. While I was getting him ready for that, I noticed that he had a red aura around his chest area and as we sat waiting for the radiographer he turned to me and said, "If I die, do you know what to do?"

Oh heck, what was I supposed to say? I asked him to tell me and explain anything I didn't understand, so he told me about his religion and all the things that should be carried out. Back on the ward, his wife and sons were waiting and as we got him into bed he started to shake for no reason and said, "I have seen an angel." Usually, you would think that seeing an angel is a good thing but in my experience it's a bad sign when very poorly people see angels – and in this instance my fears proved right. His x-ray revealed a large tumour on his lung, spreading to his bronchus.

We brought him to the nearest cubicle to the office so I could keep an extra eye on him and two days later, while I was writing the ward report, I could see something strange going on there. Adnan was holding his hands up to the sky and calling out, "Take me with you", and his family were crying and chanting so we closed all the other patients' doors. Adnan was now lying very still and I asked the family to step outside so we could see to him. He was rather sweet on one of the nurses and now he grabbed her hand and said, "I have had a message from Archangel Gabriel. They are preparing me a place to go to Jannah [Paradise] after I die." The nurse asked me, "Why can I smell baby talcum powder? It's very strong." I knew then that Adnan's life was slowly slipping away and he died peacefully two hours later with his family around him. Of course, his thirty-five extended family and friends soon arrived outside too and I'm sure that Adnan knew he was well-loved.

There are many other diseases connected to the chest and one day a man was admitted with Chronic Obstructive Pulmonary Disease (COPD); his skin was discoloured with cyanosis and he was very overweight. He was also agitated and kept pulling his oxygen mask off, and twice I caught him outside having a cigarette while the oxygen mask was still around his neck. I tried to explain that he was putting his life in danger, but he just replied, "I am dying, nurse, so don't begrudge me having a fag." It wasn't that bothering me – yes, he was dying and it would cause even more distress if we didn't allow him to smoke, but with the mask around his neck the cigarette could cause a fire!

I was giving out the teas when I noticed this gentleman had a visitor, a man wearing a black coat, so I asked the visitor if he would like a cup of tea too. He just smiled, with the most amazing blue blues that didn't quite look human, and didn't answer. I had no time to chat because we had a lot of very poorly patients on the ward so I left it and went to get the washing trolley ready, but I did comment to a colleague that I had a bad feeling about this patient. She replied, "Oh dear, I hate it when you say that!" I wondered how the man had got in, too, since the outer door was locked.

When we went back to the man's cubicle it was nearly visiting time and I could smell the familiar scent of baby talcum powder; I always smelled this or white lilies when patients were approaching death. I asked who the visitor had been but the man said he didn't know him; later, as I was writing the day's report, his wife came into the office wanting to have a word because she was concerned. "He had a visitor today but he doesn't know who it was, he thinks maybe it was a priest because he talked about bringing peace on Earth and Heaven being a beautiful place where you will be made whole again when you arrive." I could see that this could be rather disturbing. We did have a chaplain who wore black robes and visited sometimes but I knew it wasn't him.

When all the visitors had gone, I took him a hot drink and sat on the edge of the bed. He said, "The man spoke a bit soft and feminine, said he knew I was scared of dying so he just came to reassure me. His eyes were like blue diamonds and they kept getting more and more blue. I must admit I was a bit scared. He put his hand on my head and said, 'Bless you', and when I opened my eyes he'd gone."

I knew then that the 'visitor' must have been an angel in human clothes; the smell of baby powder, the blue illuminated eyes and coming in through a locked door all added up. When I told my colleagues that I thought the gentleman had been visited by an angel, one said, "We'd better get the death trolley ready then." I wasn't the only nurse to recognise these signs.

The following day I was on the late shift and as I arrived the gentleman was out of bed and greeted me. "I feel a lot better today, nurse," he said. "That priest must have done something because I can breathe better. He must have been an angel in disguise." I tried to show some enthusiasm but I knew that he wouldn't be going home, and two days later he died. But at least he had been peaceful and feeling less pain.

Some patients know exactly what is happening to them, their minds are prepared and they're calm despite everything. That's awe-inspiring to witness. Carol was one such brave lady, an ex-nurse herself. It was pouring down with rain as we were doing our rounds and as I came to her she said, "It's a beautiful sight, watching the raindrops, one I will miss enormously." She had terminal bowel cancer that had spread to her lungs and despite undergoing many chemotherapy sessions nothing had been successful. She was on strong pain relief because the cancer was relentless, and we would talk as we changed her and turned her to prevent pressure sores. She also wore a colostomy bag that needed changing frequently. I never forgot how demoralising it must be for these patients, needing a stranger to do everything for them, and I couldn't help asking God why a lady like Carol had to suffer like this, having cared for other people all her life.

Yet she was so dignified in the face of this terrible disease, which reinforced for us – as the Nursing and Midwifery Code of professional conduct says – that we should treat all patients with kindness and compassion. I had a bad back that day and was feeling very unwell, but all nurses get past the pain barrier because we know we will heal while our patients continue to suffer. I had just fed Carol by tube when I noticed that the rain had stopped so I asked her if she'd like me to open the door. We sat quietly for a moment as I thought what an amazing lady she was, coping as she did although she looked like a fragile shell.

"I just want to die and it be all over," she said calmly, "all the suffering and heartache it's bringing to my family. I want to be gone. My days are truly over, Glyn, I know I'm dying." I told her to let me know if she ever wanted to talk or ask me anything. The following day I arrived for the early shift and the night nurse was giving her report; when she got to Carol she said, "She keeps saying she has seen an angel, I think her mind is going." I just thought, 'How do you know she hasn't? If you bothered to put your knitting down you might have seen it too!'

After the general ward work was done, I took my coffee to sit with Carol and straight away she told me that, yes, she had seen an angel. I was a bit surprised because I hadn't felt any presence or smelled a fragrance as I usually do. I asked her if she would like a proper soak in the bath with bubbles and her eyes lit up. She said, "Oh, please, then I shall be lovely and clean when I go home, when they come to fetch me." Casually, I asked, "Who said you were going home?" Carol looked surprised. "The angel of course, the one I saw last night. Do you believe me?" I nodded my head and said I knew a bit about angels because my Grandma Mac had told me about them.

"It had a funny name," she began, "something like Israel, and it looked like a man and a woman at the same time. It stood at the bottom of my bed and I was scared at first, but then the room lit up with a silvery blue light for a minute. Then I was afraid the night nurse would come to see what the light was and this beautiful creature would disappear." I knew that the angel had come to comfort her; they are intelligent beings who come when

46

the time is right. "It touched my hand," she went on, "and then I had pins and needles. I thought I must be dreaming, but I closed my eyes and when I opened them the angel's wings were spread out – they looked huge, pale green, and they filled the room."

You might think that patients imagine things like this or have hallucinations because of their medication, but this was real, she hadn't dreamed it. Archangel Azrael, the angel of death, had been to see her. A couple of hours later, her husband had been sitting with her and we were just ready to go home when he knocked on the office door. "Carol wants you," he said and I knew then what was happening. I leaned over close to Carol and she took my hands, kissed them and said, "See you on the other side, girl." She quietly slipped away, holding her husband's hand.

We stayed on late to do her last offices because we were a team. Even though Carol had no hair, I left her hairband on because she was very conscious of that, it mattered to her and so it mattered to us. She had always been very smart. The porter arrived to escort her to the mortuary and as we lifted her onto the trolley we both clearly heard "Thank you." It wasn't a surprise to the porter, he had a lot of experience of hearing the dead talk to him too. A nice end for a beautiful lady.

A spirit priest made another appearance when I was working on a children's ward, doing my degree in Health Education. It was a busy city hospital housing an A&E department that was full every day and we were always expecting admissions. As part of my studies I had to devise a meal plan for a five year-old who was paralysed and could only move her mouth; she was a beautiful girl with big brown eyes and lovely black, curly hair. It's always particularly hard to see young children when they're very ill but I soon found that this girl was being cared for in a very special way.

I spent a lot of time with her, nursing her and taking her around the hospital in her pram, and she loved the meal plan I had devised. Like all children, jelly and ice cream were her favourites and she would giggle as it dripped down her dress; holding her like this broke my heart because I knew she would soon be leaving us. I was tickling her chin one day when a priest walked into the cubicle and said, "God bless you, my child." I thought he might be talking to me but then he held his arms out for the little girl and she started to call out, "Dada!"

As I looked at him I saw now that he had the most beautiful pink and green aura, and he glowed with love for this little lass; I was a bit choked up. He turned to me and said, "She will be in God's hands very soon."

I thought to myself, 'How can you say that, how do you know?' and straight away he said, "I do know. She is a beautiful and she has suffered enough, she has no life and will be happier playing with the angels." He leaned over to kiss her and with that walked out of the cubicle, his beautiful aura following him around the ward as he picked up every child and said a little prayer over them, touching their faces and blessing them. What a wonderful man, I thought, taking the time to visit all the children.

But when I turned back to my patient she had changed and looked very pale whereas she'd had rosy cheeks a few minutes before; there was also the scent of white lilies now and I knew she had deteriorated. (Why are children born like this? I've never received a clear answer though I've read that in their next lives they are privileged and will have no illness or worries.) Well, I told the doctor and chief nurse who phoned her Mum and the poor girl passed away in her mother's arms. I still often wonder who 'the priest' was.

We never knew what to expect when that Red Phone rang although we knew it was serious and we were always ready for whatever came through the door. It was especially tragic to see a small child brought into A&E after a road traffic accident. We had specially trained and excellent children's nurses in our department but there were not enough of them and, one particular day, unfortunately none were on duty. Since I was used to handling children, it fell to me to admit a child and his parents along with their three other children; they were Polish and only Dad and one of the children spoke English. The youngest was three years-old and had been sitting on his mother's knee at the front of the car without a seat belt on. The car didn't have airbags either, which would have cushioned the impact. All five occupants had injuries, the worst being the poor little boy who had glass embedded in his face, hundreds of little pieces needing to be removed.

We transferred him to the Resuscitation Room but he was deteriorating, the heart monitor bleeping away; we were all very upset but carried on trying to save him. He was a beautiful, blue-eyed lad with blond hair. Then we heard another doctor call out that one of the other children was deteriorating and we needed to bring her into Resuscitation. It was heart-breaking, seeing the children fighting for their lives.

But then something very strange happened. The young girl sat up straight and pointed to the couch the little lad was lying on, saying, "There is an angel standing over my brother!" I turned around and there was indeed an angel with the biggest wings I have ever seen, a pale green in colour, which engulfed the little lad and lifted him up, carrying his soul to Heaven. I had been so busy along with my colleagues trying to save the little boy that I hadn't noticed the angel earlier. The heart monitor showed a straight line.

There were tears streaming down the doctor's face because, he said, he had a little boy the same age, so I said I would go with him to inform the parents. Not all doctors are good at delivering bad news, it's not part of their training yet they are just expected to do it, which is unfair for someone of a sensitive nature. Nurses, on the other hand, have to put their professional head on even though their heart might be breaking or, worse, have small children themselves. We broke the news to the relatives about their son but there were no tears no screaming; I thought they must be in shock so I phoned the interpreter to come as soon as possible to confirm what the doctor had said. It was important they knew that there had to be a post-mortem because it had been an accident and further investigations were necessary.

I took the parents to see their little girl who was now sitting up and kept looking in the corner. When I asked her what was wrong she replied, "I saw an angel with big green wings take my brother to Heaven. He is safe now, isn't he, nurse?" I just nodded my head.

The police and interpreter came to see the parents and, when she realised the full extent of what had happened, the mother started screaming, "I killed my son! God will never forgive me." She knew that it was partly her fault, not wearing a seatbelt, and that would stay with her for the rest of her life. But even I was shocked when the little girl said to her mother, "An angel took my brother, I saw it take him. You will spend the rest of your life in Purgatory now." I thought that was a bit much, coming from a child, but there was some comfort in knowing that the little girl had seen the angel, and it wasn't only me. There was little or no emotional support back then for healthcare staff – we just had to get on with the job.

However much I may be used to seeing angels, sometimes even I am shocked and overawed. One Sunday morning, it was quiet until around ten o'clock when the Red Phone rang and the paramedic said they were bringing in two children who had swallowed some tablets; we didn't know what sort of tablets they were except that the bottle had had twenty in it and was now empty. We set up the Resuscitation Room and called the trauma team.

The children were two little boys, aged three and five, and it turned out that they had taken Mum's Brufen tablets. "I just went into the kitchen for five minutes and they were on the coffee table with my other pain relief tablets," she said. Sadly, we had seen quite a few overdoses like this in children over the years because these tablets – which are anti-inflammatories taken for pain relief – are bright pink and kiddies think they are sweets. (According to the Data System, 20% of child overdoses were a result of taking these.) The tablets metabolise within an hour so we had to work fast especially because the mother now said she didn't know when they had taken them.

We had to assume the worst case scenario so I started mixing the activated charcoal necessary in the sluice, when I heard a voice say gently, "The child will die." There was a very tall angel right there in front of me, not shimmering but perfectly clear, neither female nor male. The figure was stunning, in a red and gold gown with brown hair, and it towered above me. I had never seen an angel like this one and even I was quite scared.

Archangel Azrael is predominately known as 'the angel of death' but he is perhaps the kindest and gentlest of all the archangels, associated with compassion. In this way, he not only comforts and guides souls that are crossing over, he gently separates the soul from the body. Archangel Azrael is said to have many eyes and many wings.

I was asked to go and help out on a ward for young disabled people because some staff had called in sick. As I entered the ward, I had an overwhelming feeling that I should turn back and get someone else to help them, but I told myself that this was my job and I was needed. I still had a bad feeling though I couldn't understand why. The Sister and her staff were totally devoted to their patients, nothing was too much trouble and I really admired them. Moreover, the Grey Lady had never been seen on this ward, as she was on ours.

The first job was getting all the patients up, bathed and dressed, and giving them their breakfast; several patients needed to be fed by nasogastric intubation so there was a lot to do. My heart went out to these young people who had experienced some kind of trauma that had ruined their lives. One man I fed had had a motorbike accident causing brain injury and paralysis from the waist down. I introduced myself and even though he had no speech he nodded to me and I thought that while I was here I might as well wash and dress him, so I looked in his locker and saw an angel book along with motorbike magazines.

When he was settled, I just blurted out, "Would you like me to read your angel book to you?" and he smiled and nodded. It was one of those books about miracles and I thought, even though there was little hope of him recovering, reading the book might make him feel a little optimistic for the future. I had just finished the first chapter when he took hold of my hand and kissed it.

Then the orbs appeared. I noticed that he was looking up to one corner of the room and as I turned around I could see them, like coloured light bulbs all changing colour. The young man started banging his fists on the bed and calling out "Mammy!" I had read in his notes that his mother had passed over the year before – could he see her in these orbs? The other staff came running in and they saw the orbs too. "Oh my God," said one of them, "what are those?" I said that as far as I knew they were kinds of angels. The lad was staring at them and kept saying "Mammy!" Another nurse told me that he had been there two years and had never uttered a word. She laughed and said to me, "You are a miracle worker."

Well, I only wish I was. I stayed all day with the lad and had a feeling that he may pass over in the coming days so I volunteered to help again next day. I walked into his cubicle to find him laid flat and unconscious; his father was sitting with him and I had a few words with him, then as I looked again at his son there was a green glow outlining his body so I knew that he would pass over very soon. Indeed, I stood and watched in amazement as I saw his soul rising up from his body; I had been reading to this lad only twenty-four hours earlier and now the angels had taken him.

I said to his father how sorry I was but he replied, "I am not sorry. My son lived a very active life, he was a motorbike champion and a climber and a lawyer. He had the whole of his life before him but then the accident happened and he ended up like this, so I'm glad he has died. And he will be with his Mammy now. Yes, he was six feet five but he always called her his Mammy."

When the lad was taken to the mortuary, I stripped his bed and in the middle I found a small silver coin. There was also that familiar sweet scent of baby powder (talcum powder was banned on the wards).

In case I was beginning to think that angels only appear in hospital when a patient is coming to the end of their life, during one secondment in what was then called an Intensive Care Unit, for high-dependency patients, I learned that they sometimes come as healers too. I was allocated a patient with Guillain-Barré Syndrome (GBS), a rare neurological disorder where the immune system goes wrong and attacks the nerves of the body. She was a middle-aged lady in a really bad condition, yet she had always looked after herself; her nails were purple and she had some attractive piercings, although unfortunately I had to remove all these for hygienic and medical reasons – she was not at all pleased about that!

I introduced myself as her personal nurse while she was in ICU and told her to let me know if there was anything she needed. Her reply was not what I expected: "I want to die." Yes, she was very ill but all the other patients were fighting for their lives. Here we had a very uncooperative lady; she would not give any personal details about herself, she spat out medication and pulled out her cannula, the tube inserted into the body to deliver medicine. Clearly, patience was going to be needed and I can be very patient.

"Why are you being so awkward when we are trying to help you get better?" I asked kindly, but she just repeated that she wanted to die. I had an odd feeling about this woman – there was something hidden underlying all this aggression. When I walked in the next day and looked over to the lady, there were twinkling lights above her bed, orbs with faces in them and rainbow-coloured. She had deteriorated fast and now, with her eyes closed, she looked a different lady so I knew why I'd had a bad feeling about her. I felt extremely sorry for her because now the GBS had affected her speech and she had sickness and diarrhoea.

A little later I heard her crying and went over to check on her; her speech was slurred but I could make out that she was trying to say, "What have I done wrong to deserve this punishment?" My heart went out to her, she was obviously in a very dark place and only time would tell whether her condition would deteriorate further. I asked if I could do anything to help her and she mumbled, "Read to me", pointing to her locker. I was rather taken aback to find a book about angels there, so I read to her from that and enjoyed doing it.

By the end of the week she had begun to improve and her speech was returning. "I was so frightened," she told me, "I thought I would die so I prayed to the angels every day and night to make me well again." She was definitely on the mend now. "I saw an orange light last night," she went on. "Somehow, I know you will understand so I am telling you. I stared at it and it had my mother's face in it, then I knew I would be okay."

Soon after this, she asked if she could have a proper bath and I said of course she could and I would sit at the side while she washed herself. As I helped to lower her into the bath, I was shocked to see a very large tattoo on her back of coloured angels' wings. I told her how stunned I was by its beauty and she said she would like to treat me to have one myself! Sure enough, some time later a tattoo voucher arrived for me…

5

This Life Can Be Tough!

During our training, we had to do – and we had to pass – a practical ward-based test to see if we were competent to hold keys to where the dangerous drugs (DD) were kept. The Charge Nurse assessing me was a stickler and there would be no second chances with him. He asked me every possible name of each drug, what it was used for and how long it took to work, and then what the antidote was if it turned out that a patient was allergic to a particular drug. He even added his own questions, asking me where each drug was manufactured! If you failed any of your required competencies, you felt like an idiot and thought everyone would be gossiping about you behind your back, which made some of the nurses lose their self-confidence.

Well, I did pass the test; no, I am not clever, I'd stayed up every night to study after the kids went to bed. In our hospital there had to be two nurses doing the drugs round together, one of them a key-holder. Even the doctors didn't get their hands on the DD keys.

Later in my training I was seconded to Community Nursing and was to shadow the District Nurse for three months. It turned out to be an experience never to be forgotten. The first day I met my mentor I immediately liked her; she was older than me with twenty years' experience, we laughed a lot and by the end of the first week we understood each other in more ways than one. She asked me whether I was a key-holder yet because we had to give out a lot of morphine to patients. I asked her where she kept the morphine and she laughed, "It's in the patients' houses." I thought she was joking…

There are many patients who wish to stay at home instead of going to hospital to be treated and our workload was heavy. District Nurses work with very limited resources too – and little recognition or praise – and at times we had to beg, steal or borrow from doctors' surgeries. It seemed like the more work we did, the more was expected of us. For me, District Nurses are the angels of the community and deserve much more support.

We visited many patients needing palliative care and it was heart-breaking to see so many suffering as they did. Much of our time was spent giving injections, dressings wounds or bathing, and even occasionally walking the dog or feeding the cat. Hospices were new at that time too, and it was the Marie Curie nurses who had responsibility for these patients along with the District Nurses.

One patient I shall never forget was 'the lady in red', just nineteen years-old and suffering with lung cancer; she was beautiful even though she had lost her hair due to the chemotherapy treatment. Every day we visited to give her a morphine injection and every day she had her clothes laid out, ready to be dressed. She always wore her favourite colour of red – she said it gave her power – and her cherry red lipstick and Chanel perfume were ready to be applied too.

The first time I visited her and opened the bedroom door, I was met with this beautiful young lady with an angel duvet on her bed and a room full of angel ornaments including a large pair of silver angel wings above her head where she sat. Naturally, we had a good chat about angels, their different jobs and whom they choose to visit.

One very cold Tuesday we pulled up outside her house and noticed that the bedroom curtains were closed (she lived with her Mum and her sister) so at first we just thought she must be having a lie-in today; it was still early and she was our first visit. But then we looked at each other and both somehow knew there was something amiss. Her Mum came to the door and said, "She isn't well today but she still wants to see you both." I climbed the stairs with a heavy heart because the scent of death was strong. 'Why take a young lass who has her life before her?' I thought, and my Grandma Mac's words came to my mind: "God only takes the best. He looks around His place and finds what is missing, then He chooses who He wants to sit beside Him." Well, none of us can ever really know.

As we opened the bedroom door, we both felt a presence in the room and we could both see the brightly coloured splashes of auras. Our patient looked very small so I sat on the bed and asked, "Are you feeling poorly today? Would you like us to come back later?" She replied quietly, "No, I need to talk to you about angels." The District Nurse understood and said she would leave us to have a good chat and come back later, then the girl started to tell me what had happened.

"I awoke at three o'clock and when I opened my eyes there was a lady in a yellow dress sitting on my bed. The whole room looked yellow. She said, 'We have a place ready for you, do not be afraid.'" Even I was a bit shocked by how calmly and clearly she described the meeting. "She held my hand," the girl went on, "and said she was my personal angel. So I need you both to do something for me." I replied that of course we would do anything she wanted within reason.

"In my bottom drawer is some red underwear, red shoes and dress and a red knitted hat my sister made for me. When I have died, please can you dress me in those clothes, and put my red lipstick and Chanel No. 5 perfume on? It's all set out ready for you on the dressing table." I agreed of course, and then she took hold of my hand and kissed it. "I'll let you know what it's like in Heaven," she smiled.

I left with a heavy heart and the phone rang at nine o'clock that evening; it was the District Nurse telling me that our 'lady in red' had passed over and asking me to go with her to do the last offices. It's usually considered disrespectful to talk at these moments but this time felt different, so the District Nurse and I did talk to this beautiful girl about angels and what a pleasure it had been to know her. It was no surprise that one of the songs at her funeral was 'Lady in Red'.

You might have noticed – and perhaps it's not too surprising – that most of these accounts of angelic encounters have involved female patients. Perhaps women are more likely to be interested in angels or be sensitive to their presence? But it isn't always so and a memorable story (with more than one surprising twist) involved two young men, neither of whom had any interest in the supernatural before they arrived on my ward. This particular ward had a very good atmosphere, all the nurses got on well and we made sure of going the extra mile for our patients to give them the best possible care.

A young man was admitted to the ward with haemoptysis, the coughing of blood from the respiratory tract usually the result of a chest infection like pneumonia. He was only thirty years-old, a heavy smoker, and was due to have a bronchoscopy to find out the cause of his trouble; this can also be a sign of cancer and for some reason we were getting quite a few younger people coming for investigations related to cancer (I myself had cervical cancer when I was twenty-nine.) This man was quite emaciated with a shrunken face and I felt so sorry for him when I saw his very dark grey and murky aura. I admitted him and made him comfortable and told him he would be sharing a room with another young man; when the second young man arrived soon afterwards it was strange to see that he was around the same age as his room-mate and looked to be in the same predicament.

These two men got on really well together, sharing their experiences and chatting and laughing with other patients. The day of their investigations arrived and they both went off to have their bronchoscopies: the notes told me later that they both had lung cancer and they were both beginning to look very ill. Usually on a summer evening patients would sit on the veranda for a chat (and even have a smoke!) but this was a grim day on the ward. It's a shock to be told you have cancer especially when you are so young, so today things were very quiet and most of the patients slept.

One of the men began to deteriorate and needed strong pain relief. Back then we had a mixture called 'Brompton's Cocktail' made up by the pharmacy, its ingredients including morphine and, sometimes, gin and chlorpromazine (an antipsychotic) to counteract nausea. We also had Guinness sent in by the landlord of a local public house for the patients and unsurprisingly this pain relief was the highlight of the day for some patients! How things have changed. The young man became very distressed, though, when I gave him his medication, saying, "How can I die? I have three young children."

The doctor and nurses tried to reassure him that he could be treated but he just cried pitifully. Each evening around eight o'clock, when the patients were settling down after their visitors had left, we did a 'bowel and bums' round to ensure that patients didn't get pressure sores and to deal with the constipation often caused by their medication. We never minded this as it gave us time to talk with the patients while… well, I won't go into details.

When we got to this young man his room-mate was sitting holding his hand, which I thought was surprising as they hardly knew each other. They were both laughing with tears streaming down their faces, so I asked, "What's so funny, have you had an extra dose of Brompton's Cocktail?" The reply was quite a shock. "No, a weird man just came into the room while we were talking. He was wearing a blue gown and had really golden hair, looked out of place here so we didn't know what to say to him. He put his hands on both of ours and then walked out without saying anything. And he had these piercing blue eyes – like yours, nurse."

"Right then," I laughed, "I'll remember you said that about my eyes the next time Guinness is given out." But I walked out

59

of the room later with a heavy heart and a bad feeling about these two men. Obviously, no such 'weird man' could have come in, there had been an angelic visit. The following morning neither of them got up for breakfast because they felt too poorly. One of them said to me, "Why do you wear a different dress to the Night Nurse? She had a big red cross on the front." I swore silently to myself – the Grey Lady was on the prowl again, visiting the patients when they are ready to pass over. She always brought the scent of white lilies too, the perfume of death.

After this, the two young men became very close friends, whispering and talking to each other all the time; if one went to the toilet, the other waited outside, and they sat at the dinner table together with no-one else. It was becoming a bit creepy, like suddenly they were soulmates (in a friendly way) and they even spoke for one another when the nurses asked questions.

Now, at that time we had an occupational therapist who helped the patients make things, to keep them busy and help their mood, and the two young men said they wanted to make wooden crosses to be put on their graves. The therapist became very upset, though, and asked why; she didn't think it was 'appropriate'. They told her that a man – they thought it was probably a man – had come to see them and he'd been wearing a wooden cross that they both liked the look of. She said she wouldn't allow that.

I told her I had seen psychiatric patients doing woodwork in occupational therapy so why couldn't these two men join in? They were very poorly and felt they needed to do this, it was important to them. But she wouldn't budge so I went to the boss and told him the tale; he said he would come over himself to see the men and ask someone else to help them make their crosses. Result! Two days later, they had their crosses.

On the third day I came on duty and they were both in bed, having haemorrhaged during the night. One of the men said, "That strange bloke came to see us again last night and next thing we know we are coughing our guts up. Who is he?" I replied, fingers crossed, that he was just someone who visits patients sometimes, although I was sure now that it was an angel and theses two men would soon pass over. Only a couple of hours later I went back to their room and saw that the ethereal silver cord of one of the men was broken; the other man was holding his hand, sobbing. We were gently removing him to another cubicle so we could do the last offices when we saw a flash of brilliant light in the room, a holy presence that had just left us.

The second man was inconsolable and he deteriorated so quickly that he passed over too the next day. As I was doing the last offices for him, I put on his wristband and stood back in shock: it showed the same date of birth as his room-mate. I thought we'd got the wrong date so went back to check their notes, realising that they had both been born on the same day in the same hospital. How uncanny was that? Their relatives promised to put the wooden crosses in the Garden of Remembrance beside one another. And I bet the two men are up in Heaven having a good old chat. I hope they've met up with their blue-robed, golden-haired visitor again.

Some of the allocations during my training were far more challenging than others, and we all have to understand that there are many patients in very distressing circumstances who need and deserve help. At least I was privileged to know that, however extreme their cases seem to us, these patients also receive angelic support. That knowledge can help us all to be more compassionate.

With my friend Joan, I entered a certain high security hospital for the criminally insane, built in the early twentieth century, with some trepidation. Joan was one of those people you could totally trust to help you out and she had a fantastic personality; we had laughed and cried together throughout the A&E trauma course. The Charge Nurse welcomed us and said, "Every door is locked as we go through it. And never turn your back on a patient – some of them may appear very calm but in the blink of an eye…" We began to wonder what on Earth we were letting ourselves in for and hoped he was just being a bit dramatic. He went on, "We have picked out two patients for you to work with. They have both killed people but they're not as violent as some of the others. Still, I suggest you work with them within view of other people."

"Do you have a church here?" I asked him. Joan looked quizzically at me and I winked back. A voice had told me where to find Dora; moreover, for me, a church is a place of forgiveness and people do seem to be able to open up better there. The Charge Nurse said in surprise, "How did you know your patient was in the church?"

She was sitting with three other ladies and I could see a grey orb around her head, although there was a beautiful fragrant scent when she turned around. I asked her if it was okay for me to sit there and talk with her and she replied, "I'm the one who killed her two daughters. Do you really want to talk to me after knowing that?" I said that, yes, I did and the Charge Nurse gave me a strange look as if to say he couldn't understand why anyone would want to spend time with someone like her. "Just watch out then," he said, "because she tells lies. Anyway, it will have to be tomorrow because there aren't enough staff for someone to sit with you." I did think he was being a bit overprotective; she was seven stone and very nervous, what was she going to do to me? Still, rules are rules, especially in a place like this.

Next day, Dora was waiting in the church along with a female nurse. She had brought a photograph of her two girls; both had blonde hair and blue eyes and both were disabled by Spina Bifida. I said they looked lovely and Dora's aura immediately changed to a dark pink. "People say I'm a monster," she began, "but if they only knew the real circumstances…" She had been caring for the girls on her own in very poor conditions, trying to feed them by tube, while her husband did nothing to help. He would shout at Dora and hit her, blaming her for the girls' disability because she'd been unfaithful in the past. He wouldn't touch the girls and said, "The Devil made them." To Dora the girls were still beautiful but the stress was just too much. "They would just stare at the wall, they never responded, and I prayed that just once they would say 'Mama' but they couldn't."

The priest came over with a glass of water for her but she threw it back at him, saying he was trying to poison her. He simply walked away calmly, but now I realised why Dora needed to have an escort.

She told me that she had strangled the girls and then tried to kill herself because she wanted to die with them. At that moment, I smelled a strong fragrance of roses and turned round to see a man with white hair and beard sitting quietly in a corner; he wore a purple robe and a golden cloak and light seemed to be shining from him. Then I remembered that I had seen a portrait of him in my Grandma Mac's house: it was Archangel Melchizedek, head of the archangels and an Ascended Master, sometimes called 'the angel of spiritual evolution'. Why was he here?

Dora was not sorry for what she'd done, she thought she had saved the children from a cruel world. "I prayed every day to the angels to take them but nothing happened and I prayed to God to forgive me." All the while, Archangel Melchizedek sat in the corner listening and watching, and then he spoke to me in my mind: "She will soon be with her babies." Then he disappeared.

I was astonished. How could that happen when she was supervised constantly? I hugged her before I left, with a very bad feeling about her. The next week I returned to the hospital and asked to see Dora but the Charge Nurse said, "She's gone. She died of a brain haemorrhage on Sunday." So that's why the archangel had come, to take care of her. Was she now with her children?

It's so difficult for any of us to judge another's actions when we don't know what they've been through. Some people have such difficult lives and their minds suffer. Even if we can't understand or accept why people like Dora do what they do, the angels still have love for them.

Another psychiatric hospital I worked in was ultra-modern; the patients were allowed to go out and they had their own cosy rooms with tea and coffee whenever they wanted. They could roam the corridors too and because the staff didn't wear uniforms you couldn't distinguish between them. But the walls were an awful yellowy-brown and the Staff Room was a mess, with crisp packets and sandwich wrappers overflowing the bins. I was there with my colleague Cath. As we arrived, she said, "If you tell the Charge Nurse you hear voices, he'll section you. And if you don't share your sandwiches with me I'll tell him!" I laughed and begged her to keep quiet. "Okay," she said, "but only if you do me a reading." She would go far in her nursing career, she was young and fit and she could face anything.

I was allocated to the Young Persons section where a tired-looking male nurse introduced himself as my mentor. After five minutes sitting in the Staff Room as he told me about the patients I would be seeing, I wanted to shake him because he seemed so depressed. I asked him how long he'd been working here and he sighed, "Too long." But I knew that psychiatric nurses are amazing for the way they handle their patients; you have to be a very special person to do this work. We were asked to choose the patients to shadow and I chose Elena.

She was eighteen years old, bipolar and anorexic and had been at the hospital for three months but didn't seem to be getting better. I suggested we went to her room for a chat and when she opened the door I was taken aback: the wall was covered with pictures of angels and God with cherubim at his feet, and there was also a picture of Lucifer. She asked, "Do you like my collage? I made it before I became ill but the staff here think it's terrible to include Lucifer. What do you think?" I replied that not everything in this world is sweetness and light, and every angel, fallen or not, has a job to do. It made her happy that I understood her thoughts, but then she shocked me by saying, "I pray every night to the angels to let me die so I can meet them."

Well, I tried to reassure her that she was talented and beautiful

and should make the most of her life. Back then, I didn't understand mental illness very well (this lass didn't eat because 'voices
in her head' told her not to) yet I knew that Spirit must have led
me to her and I would try to help her all I could. After all, we
had angels in common.

The bell rang for tea so we went to get some food and sit outside for a chat. She came to the table with a plate piled high with
sausage rolls, scotch eggs, sandwiches and crisps. "It's for both
of us," she said. "I know that you're my friend now." This was
progress and somehow, I thought, the pattern of anorexia nervosa
didn't quite fit Elena even though she said her favourite food was
jelly "Because it's slippery and easy to vomit back." She nibbled
at a meat sandwich and half a cake as I saw her aura improving
to a lovely pink. When the Charge Nurse came by, she told him,
"Look, I've eaten more than yesterday."

Elena had become interested in angels when she was ten years-
old and saw one at her grandad's bedside when he died. She had
been close to her grandad, going for walks in the woods with him
where he would point out the flowers and birds and say, "Look
up to the sky, you might see an angel looking down." The angel
she did see had a white robe with a golden belt. I told her that I
knew some things about angels and if she ate her sausage roll I
would tell her about them. We were developing a rapport and I
told her a few of my stories.

"I have a secret I want to tell you," she said. "I've seen another
angel here, standing at the end of my bed. It had a pink frock
on and around its body it was shining pink, and it had strange
eyes too." I recognised her description as Archangel Chamuel,
the angel who comes to transform someone's life by building
their confidence with the pink ray of love. "Do you want to get
better?" I asked her, when I'd told her about Chamuel. "I'm sure
you can, but it's up to you." She skipped away and seemed a lot
happier than when we'd first met. I decided to find out more and
next day brought two books and a rose quartz crystal in the shape
of an angel for her.

The following day I was met by the Charge Nurse, who said, "Can I have a word?" Oh no, I thought, I'm in trouble. "Who are you?" he went on, "Some kind of miracle worker sent down from Heaven to convert people? None of the therapy that Elena had has worked, then you come along and in one day she's eating properly and not vomiting it back." I told him that all we did was talk and suggested that he ask her to make another collage to display on the wall, because she wanted to do Art and Design at college. He said he would try to support her. And as I walked down the corridor to Elena's room there was a lovely smell of fresh toast!

I gave her the rose quartz crystal and said, "When you feel down, use the crystal to call your angel and ask him to help you." She started to cry, then said, "There's something I have to tell you, let's go outside... Last night, I took down the picture of Lucifer and prayed to the Archangel Chamuel to help me get better. I woke up around three o'clock and it felt as though someone had their arms around me – then the room started to glow pink, flashing on and off like a light bulb. A face appeared in the light, the same face I'd seen before, and I heard a voice say, 'God bless you.' Then it disappeared and I fell asleep soon afterwards. This morning I started to paint again."

She showed me a beautiful picture of Archangel Chamuel with wings outspread in silver and pink. When I showed the Charge Nurse he pinned it up on the wall and told everyone that Elena would do paintings for them for a small charge to cover the cost of the paper and paint. She was really happy now and I had a lump in my throat.

I asked her to paint my own special angel for me. Archangel Jophiel is the angel of wisdom; his name means 'the beauty of God' and his ray is often called 'the ray of sunshine'. He is important to me because when I was diagnosed with cervical cancer I had a serious operation that prevented me having more children. Nothing could shift my depression, even though my husband Frank and mother-in-law Flora were amazingly kind. Then one day I sat in the garden and could smell roses – we didn't have any at that time – and I heard a voice say, "You are well." I turned around to see a figure standing there in a yellow gown holding a book; his eyes were a light brown edged with yellow and he just said "Jophiel" before vanishing. From that day there was an instant change in me. He'd come when I was in shock, having had a severe illness, but before long I went back to work.

Elena listened carefully and said, "I promise you I will do well when I get out of here." Then I taught her this meditation to do every night before sleep:

> *Hold the rose quartz crystal angel in your hand, sitting quietly in your chair. Take five deep breaths, focusing on the angel.*
> *Ask Archangel Chamuel to send you healing and release your anxieties and tensions from you, and send them out into the universe.*
> *See yourself surrounded by pink light, breathe it in deeply and then blow it out, releasing your emotions.*
> *Take one more deep breath, hold it in and imagine it as pink, and let it flow throughout your body.*
> *Then thank Archangel Chamuel for guiding you.*

She did this ritual every night and each day there was an improvement; she was only eating small amounts but she was keeping it down, she became brighter mentally and started joining in with activities and helping other patients. On my last day at the hospital, I went to find her and she had her bags packed to go home; her Mum and Dad said to me, "We held little hope of her ever getting well so thank you and the staff for what you have done."

"I shall never forget you, nurse," she said. "You helped me to be strong." I smiled, "We did good, didn't we?" But all I'd really done was listen to her and believe in her; it was Archangel Chamuel who had brought the healing. When she had gone, the

Charge Nurse gave me a picture that Elena had left for me. It was Archangel Jophiel and not only did he have the book in his hands, he held a rose quartz crystal too.

Many years later, she came into A&E with her husband and two children because one child had fallen off a wall. She squealed when she saw me and gave me the biggest hug. "All these years and we meet again," she said. "I can never repay you for helping me to meet the angels."

Here is another meditation for angelic guidance:

Sit in a comfortable chair, making sure that you won't be disturbed. Light a candle, close your eyes and focus on your breathing, allowing it to become slower and deeper. Breathe in and out five times, releasing the tension from your body. Invoke Archangel Michael and ask for his gift of empowerment and love by activating his blue ray of Divine will and power within you.

Focus your awareness on your heart, placing your hand there and feeling a flame growing bigger, brighter and stronger. You will begin to feel a tingling and a warmth in your body.

Visualise the blue ray spiralling up your spine and into your crown.

The blue ray surrounds you now, protecting you.

Allow your consciousness to travel upwards through a tunnel of light, emerging into a pyramid of light that is your higher self, your soul.

Here you will meet the angels sitting around a crystal table. Tell them exactly how you have become empowered by Archangel Michael's blue ray. Thank them for allowing you to communicate with them.

Allow the process to unfold naturally, slowly returning to your normal consciousness and opening your eyes. Drink some water.

There were many times in my career when I and the other staff feared for our patients, some of whom were in desperate situations – not just medically but with such sad lives that they didn't seem to have the will to survive. On the other hand, miracles do happen with the help of Spirit and the angels.

It was a lovely summer evening and I was doing an A&E trauma course in a small hospital that wasn't busy. The senior nurse, who was very calm and unfazed by anything, was instructing me in the art of triage; she told me that the tricky part of triage is deciding between who is at death's door and who just shouts the loudest. "Right," she said after a while, "the next patient is yours."

The porter wheeled in a very obese lady who was sweating, had a sore throat and joint pain, and was smelling strongly of alcohol. This was not going to be easy and I had to get it right. I asked her what she thought the problem was and she replied, hardly able to speak, "I don't know, nurse." I looked at her throat first and immediately had to take a step back in shock when I saw bulging oesophageal varices (which occurs in alcoholism). This was serious. I called the senior nurse over, who seemed annoyed at having to leave her coffee, and she looked at the patient's throat and asked the lady how much she drank in a normal day. The answer was two bottles of wine and a bottle of cider! I had a terrible premonition that this lady was in deep trouble.

Suddenly I saw a spirit man appear beside the lady and he spoke in my mind, "I am waiting for her." The senior nurse looked at me oddly – had she sensed something? – and said we'd get a doctor to look at the patient, but then the lady coughed, stared towards the ceiling, and vomited bright red blood all over both of us. We rang the emergency bell and doctors came flying into the room, one holding a piece of toast and a coffee.

Our patient was transferred to the Resuscitation Room where an electrocardiogram showed that she was in heart failure. The spirit man was still with us, holding her hand and not leaving her side which is usually a sign that a patient is about to pass over. Somehow, however, I felt that she wouldn't. I watched as the doctor moved around the lady from her head to her feet, walking straight through the spirit.

I carefully placed five small phials of blood in a row for the doctor to use and watched in astonishment as, a minute later, they toppled over like dominoes as the spirit man flicked them. When I looked back from clearing them up, there was a beautiful, gentle angelic figure in shining robes standing beside the spirit. She spoke softly, "It's not her time." In a moment, the cardiac monitor changed its rhythm back to normal and the bleeding stopped. Doctors and nurses looked at one another in amazement, all thinking, 'How on Earth did that happen?'

Even that wasn't the end of the spiritual drama, though. The lady was stabilised and the senior nurse and I were just taking her along the corridor to Intensive Care when we both heard a voice, coming out of nowhere, say, "That's my Mummy." The patient gave an almighty scream and the blood came gushing out again. I thought that this time she really would pass over and I watched for the silver cord breaking, but somehow the doctors got things under control and it didn't happen. The spirits left us to it.

A week later, I called in to see how she was getting on and was happy to see that she was improving. But her mood was very low. She told me – by writing on a pad because she was being fed by a tube and couldn't speak – that she'd had two daughters, but one had died three months before and the other one walked out ten years ago. "That's why I'm an alcoholic," she wrote. "I have nothing to live for." I got her to tell me her daughter's name and some idea of where she lived, and later contacted Social Services to see whether they could find the daughter. Yes, she was actually living not far away in the next village so the lady asked me to write to her, letting her know that her sister had died (and I added that her mother was in hospital).

When I called in to see her again a few days later there had been no word but, as I stood up to leave, a voice behind me said, "Hello, Mum." The floodgates opened and a near-death experience had reunited them.

"No more alcohol for me, nurse," she told me as she was discharged. "I'm going to live with my daughter and my two grandchildren." She looked at me quizzically and went on, "I know my husband was holding my hand when I came in, and I thought he'd come for me. You saw him, didn't you?" I laughed and admitted it, telling her that he'd knocked the blood phials over too. "Yes, that would be him," she said. "He liked to get people's attention."

6

What I Have Learned

Throughout my life, I have been learning about – and meeting with – angels. As the stories in this book reveal, many other people have these encounters too. It is not an everyday experience, though, so perhaps it will be helpful if I share my beliefs here along with some practices that can bring us all into a closer relationship with those in higher worlds who care for us.

The most common question I am asked is, "Does everyone have a guardian angel?" Yes, we do! These angels are, if you like, the guardians of the blueprints of our lives, the experiences we have agreed to go through before we were born. Our guardian angels love us and want the best for us, always on our side, and their job is to guide and teach us. They are there to protect us, too, but sometimes we need to go through difficult challenges or illness so that we can grow on the spiritual path. Our guardian angels (who come from what is called 'the Seventh Dimension') allow these things to happen to ensure that our spiritual development progresses, and they are always there to offer comfort in our hour of need.

The law of 'ask and you will receive' when you need help is true – even if that help doesn't always come quite as we expected! There is always a direct link to our guardian angels and over time, as we reach out to them, we become more familiar with their energy. They may even show themselves to us in dreams or visions, by a fragrance or other sign. So how can we contact them? This is what I do:

> *Firstly, find a quiet place and time where you won't be disturbed, sit comfortably and relax. Take several slow, deep breaths, breathing out your anxieties to the universe.*
> *Light a candle of your choice. I usually have a blue or green candle or one with the fragrance of lavender. Blue is for Archangel Michael, who brings protection, green is for Archangel Raphael and for enlightenment; sometimes I choose yellow for Archangel Jophiel, who is my favourite because she brings me joy and strength. You may like to put on some soft, celestial music too.*

Angels like to work with the special energy of crystals so you may like to have one or two with you. Which ones to choose?

Angelite	This is the crystal for guidance and spiritual awareness, and for connecting with the angelic realms. Its qualities are peace and tranquility for the mind.
Rutilant Quartz	The cosmic healer crystal. It has golden threads running through it, making us think of an angel's hair.
Celestine	Called 'the stone of Heaven', its beautiful light blue attracts angels and links strongly with the Guardians of Light who guide the cosmos. It has power to calm the emotions.

Rock Quartz	Known as 'the master healer' because it clears any negative energies around us and calms the mind.
Amethyst	This beautiful purple gem is the crystal for guidance.
Aura Aqua Quartz	A beautiful crystal used during challenging circumstances.
Lapis Lazuli	This is a protector and motivator.

Focus on your crown, the spiritual centre, and hold your crystal. Now ask the angels to protect you and to come forward and reveal themselves: Archangel Michael gives protection but you can ask your personal angel to send a white light of protection. You may visualise this in your mind or even see it in the room with you; don't be afraid, for angels come with white light.

Ask your guardian angel their name and be open to receive any intuition or other signs from them; be willing to listen and put into practice what your angel suggests. If I am not sure about something I speak to my guardian angel and say, "Please can I have your guidance? I need your help with this problem and my heart is open to your guidance." Usually a clear thought will then come into my mind, like "Yes, do it" or "Definitely not!" The more you work like this with angels, the easier it becomes to connect.

It is important that we always thank our guardian angels for their love and for the insights they give us. As time goes on we recognise that we have an important connection with them, we are evolving spiritually and beginning to get more information and messages through meditations, visualisations, dreams and everyday signs. Then when you are ready, allow yourself to come back slowly to normality and drink a glass of water as you may feel a little spaced out or overwhelmed with what you have experienced. But it's wonderful to know that you have connected with your own guardian angel and perhaps now know their name. This is my prayer of thanks:

Thank you, my angels, for coming near
and bringing peace to all, especially those most dear.
Please hear the prayers I say today,
bring me hope and guide my way.
Show me in dreams what I should know
so I can walk within your glow.
Thank you.

Here are some of the archangels along with the crystals especially associated with them:

Michael   The deep lavender crystal amethyst, a calming meditation stone that also helps the development of psychic abilities.

Gabriel   The orange carnelian, a wonderful crystal to give you confidence.

Uriel   The beautiful red ruby, called 'the lord of gems', improves self-esteem and works with the higher self to heal old problems.

Raphael   The green emerald creates harmony, helps us to achieve balance in our lives and brings healing.

Raziel   Clear quartz, the master healing stone, for clarity and insight.

Zadkiel   A gold-flecked cobalt blue, the lapis lazuli crystal opens the third eye and higher self for connecting with Spirit.

Azrael   Green tourmaline is known as a rejuvenating crystal and it brings a calmness to the mind.

Haniel   Labradorite has beautiful iridescent colours, a crystal of connection to expand the consciousness.

Chamuel   Pink tourmaline helps to open the heart to love and connection with spiritual energy.

Metatron   Ocean jasper, a beautiful pink stone, has healing properties and its soft, loving energy helps with the karmic ties of life.

Angels often come to us during the altered consciousness of dreams, so it's helpful to reach out to them with a prayer at night, thanking them for protecting us and our family and asking for guidance. Often, we don't remember all the details of our dreams but we can recognise an angelic presence by, for example, the scent of white roses or especially vibrant colours. Angels may show us numbers, symbols or even appear as themselves to deliver a message to us; this could be about, say, someone who has wronged us, suggesting that we forgive them, or showing us where to find valuable items that we've lost. Keeping a journal of angelic dreams makes the connection stronger and helps us to improve our understanding of dreams in time. Don't worry if you can't remember a dream; if it's important it will be brought back to mind or your angel will give you a nudge with some other signs during the day.

You may have heard about angelic 'rays', the special colours of light associated with each archangel. Indeed, it is by these colours that we can identify which angel is bringing a message to us, perhaps in a dream.

Ruby Ray   This is the ray of Archangel Uriel, the angel of peace, whose name means 'light of God'. He is very powerful and is often depicted holding a scroll that contains all your information, past and future. Uriel appears to those who have lost their way in life, his ruby ray illuminating the pathway to a better life. He helps us to connect with the Divine and brings peace to the world. Also, as red is the first colour of the spectrum, a dream where red is dominant is summoning us to explore a new topic.

Yellow Ray   Jophiel is the archangel of wisdom whose name means 'beauty of God'. Her yellow wisdom flame clarifies mental perception and brings inspiration and illumination of the soul, strengthening the connection with the higher self. She is the angel of creativity so this ray helps us to develop fresh approaches to life, restoring the vitality we might have lost. A dream of Archangel Jophiel encourages us to share our wisdom with others.

Blue Ray   Sapphire blue is Archangel Michael's ray. He is the protector of humanity and the 'commander in chief' of all the archangels, leading the heavenly forces against evil. The blue ray represents the will and power of God. Michael is a warrior, carrying a sapphire blue sword, and he empowers us to bring peace on Earth and to seek the higher truth. If you see this ray, it means you will be able to face any problem because Archangel Michael is on your side.

Green Ray   This comes with Archangel Raphael, the healer who comes to enfold and smooth away all our stress and negative emotions. There is a cleansing fragrance to his robes and he has the most beautiful golden wings. If you see the green ray it means that Raphael brings healing and spiritual support.

Indigo Ray   The ray of Archangel Raziel, the keeper of mysteries whose name means 'secrets of God'. He helps us to focus on personal issues and self-knowledge. If we dream of the indigo ray, Archangel Raziel is telling us that we have psychic gifts and our knowledge of spiritual mysteries is being developed.

Orange Ray   Here is the messenger, Archangel Gabriel, who announces important news. She is sometimes seen wearing white with a golden belt but is recognised by the trumpet she carries and her fragrance of white roses. Archangel Gabriel is also the one who escorts souls to Heaven, leaving an orange and white aura as she ascends. If you are fortunate to dream of Gabriel or experience her orange ray, then you are being encouraged to spread the word of Spirit to the world.

Violet Ray   The highest vibration in the 'rainbow' of rays is that of Archangel Zadkiel, the angel of mercy and benevolence known as 'the holy one'. He is often portrayed holding a dagger (he was the angel who stopped Abraham sacrificing his son Isaac in the Old Testament) with which he cuts away emotional problems. If this violet flame comes to you in a dream, it means you can help others in their quest for spiritual knowledge and Zadkiel will give you psychic protection.

White Ray   Archangel Metatron is the angel of writers and keeper of the Akashic Records that record our souls' incarnations. Metatron has great power to bring spiritual growth to us, cleansing and balancing our emotions. (People who have near-death experiences often encounter Archangel Metatron.) It is rare to dream of the brilliant white ray of Archangel Metatron so if you do it is a very special moment.

The word 'angel' is derived from the Greek word for 'messenger' and, indeed, these celestial beings act as a bridge between Heaven and Earth, appearing when we need help, protection and guidance. Just like us, angels belong to families each having a particular vocation. There are nine classes – or 'choirs' – of angels, divided into three 'spheres' with the first of these being closest to God.

Sphere One

The first sphere holds the highest order of angels, the *Seraphim*, which means 'enflamed' with the divine fire, love and light. They are sometimes called 'the burning ones'. Being closest to God, they continually sing His praise and radiate pure love, destroying the shadows of darkness. A colourful mosaic of one of these six-winged angels can be seen in the Basilica of St Marco in Venice, Italy.

The *Cherubim* were sent to Earth with the greatest of tasks as powerful guardians holding the energies of the Sun, Moon and stars. Originally, they were depicted as having four wings and four faces, but have become seen in popular culture as chubby, winged babies. Their ruler is Cassiel, the archangel of solitude and tears.

Thrones, or 'many-eyed ones', carry out God's decisions. They are angelic beings shaped like tiny coloured orbs and they make God's will known to the ministering angels. Some say that the Virgin Mary was one of these.

Sphere Two

The *Dominions* oversee the lower angelic realm, receiving their orders from the *Seraphim*, maintaining the cosmos and keeping order. Helping to integrate the spiritual and physical realms, occasionally a *Dominion* will appear to mortals. They are recognised by a sceptre or orb carried in the left hand and a golden staff in the right hand.

The *Virtues*, also known as 'the shining ones', are the miracle workers on Earth associated with heroic acts and courage. They are ruled over by Archangel Gabriel, the angel of love and families. Jesus was accompanied by two *Virtues* when he ascended to Heaven.

Also referred to as 'karmic lords', the *Powers* protect our souls, keep the universe in balance, and have the task of preventing fallen angels from taking over. They are angels of birth and death who also oversee the distribution of power to mankind. The archangel related to power is Chamuel, also the finder of lost objects.

Sphere Three

At the head of the third hierarchy are the *Principalities* who guide towns and cities, countries and sacred sites, protecting them against evil. They also lead religions to the paths of truth and are ruled by Haniel, who works with group energies and communications.

Archangels are known as the ruling or chief angels, carrying most of God's messages to us on Earth. Powerful leaders in the divine army, they fight against darkness and serve as 'the guardians of guardians' (such as religious leaders).

Finally, we have the *Angels* who are the lowest order but closest to humanity, bringing messages to all mankind and helping in many ways to bring greater harmony to our lives. They are often referred to as 'guardian angels'.

Angels do not have gender as we know it and most of them appear androgynous, yet there do seem to be some specifically feminine archangels, called 'the archeiai'. For instance there is Lady Haniel whose name means 'grace of the goddess' and who is the angel of the Moon, of the womb and spiritual rituals. Lady Ariel, the 'lioness of the goddess' is the angel of strength, of nature and of magic.

You might have heard of 'fallen angels' too, usually referring to the bad boy himself, Lucifer. He was once an archangel but led a revolt against God, refusing to bow down before Adam, His new creation, and so was banished from Heaven and condemned along with his fellow rebels to 'hellfire' forever. The story of his fall is related in the apocryphal Book of Adam and Eve, and even mentioned in the Koran.

We do not really have to be concerned about him because there are far too many good angels who protect us in every way they can, although there are quite a few in Lucifer's army. There is the wild one Amduscias who presents himself as a lovely white unicorn, followed closely by Beelzebub who is known as 'the prince of demons' and by Gaap, who appears as a man with bats' wings!

7

I'm Not The Only One!

When I was a trainee nurse I was still very unsure of myself and felt inadequate; I looked for jobs to do but all I heard was, "You can't do this, you can't do that…" So I cowered in the background while more senior nurses ran in and out of the treatment rooms. Eventually one day, Sister noticed me and said that one lady was dying so I could go and sit with her; she was doubly incontinent so I should wear gloves and an apron. It seemed to me a bit disrespectful to sit with a dying patient wearing this protective equipment so I took them off and put them to one side. The lady was in a single cubicle at the end of the ward, isolated away from other patients (which also annoyed me!).

This lady had been a nurse, in fact a Red Cross nurse during the Second World War. Her cubicle was full of Get Well cards and bunches of flowers, but even these couldn't mask the scent of approaching death. All the signs were there, the whitening of the nose and the shrunken face, the plucking of bedsheets… yet she was smiling and holding her hands as though someone were there beside her. And what had been a throwaway suggestion to 'go and sit with that dying lady' in order to give me something to do turned out to be one of the best experiences I ever had of the privilege of being with patients at the end of their lives.

"I am a widow," she said. "When I was a Red Cross nurse I worked in war-torn countries tending wounded soldiers. I loved them all but there was one special one. He had been involved in an explosion and had his leg blown off, but as soon as I saw him I knew I would marry him, it was love at first sight.

"One day," she continued, "I was tending to a soldier who had gunshot wounds when I glanced up and across the ward was a soldier who was dying. There was a strange light at the side of the bed – we only had small lamps – and I was mesmerised by what I saw, a shimmering figure looking down at the man. It wasn't just me, we all saw this angelic figure in a greenish gown with golden wings, and the next thing we knew we heard a 'whoosh' and watched the man's soul rise up from his body."

I was fascinated by her story but I could tell, partly because of my nursing knowledge but also by my spiritual intuition, that she was deteriorating fast and would pass over in the next few hours. She asked me if I believed in angels so of course I was able to say that I knew of many angels who come to support and protect us. "I saw my own angel last night," she said. "It said 'You will have peace, there is a special place for you.'"

As she was speaking I could smell the strong fragrance of white roses that Archangel Gabriel leaves and I could feel a presence and a sense of calm in the room. She was going to pass over very soon so I told her I would go to fetch some morphine for her pain. When morphine is given to patients it must be administered by a qualified nurse, checked twice, and two nurses attend the patient. When we opened the cubicle door we could both see that there was someone sitting with the lady holding her hand, a figure wearing a long blue robe with blond hair, who then vanished before our eyes.

"I see you had a visitor," I said quietly to the lady. "Yes, nurse, he came for me," she said. I sat and held her hand as she gently passed over and the other nurse with me, who was religious, closed the door and said a prayer to the angels for her. I had great respect for that nurse all through my career.

I had another, rather unorthodox, experience of a Red Cross nurse when I was an inexperienced auxiliary. The staff on a ward for young disabled patients had called in sick and I was asked to go and help the only nurse left there. We had put the patients to bed and things were quiet when the nurse came to me with car keys in her hand and said, "Won't be long, I'm just going to get my husband's supper."

"You can't leave me alone here," I replied nervously. She laughed, "You'll be all right, you have Lizzie for company." Who was Lizzie? A minute later, as I stood by the window watching the nurse walk across to her car, one of the patients, Tom, shouted out that he needed the toilet. I was unsure what to do and afraid I would lose my job, when another young patient with Down's syndrome put his arm around me and said, "The nurse with the Red Cross is on the ward, shall I tell her to see to Tom?" I said that I was the only nurse here but he pointed along the corridor where the Grey Lady was walking up to other end.

I went along to Tom's room, to help him with the toilet, and the Grey Lady had got there ahead of me. She was wearing a beige coat over an old-fashioned uniform with a large red cross on the front – and Tom could see her too! "Look who's here, nurse," he said, before turning to the ghost and shouting, "I hate you!" Then he picked up a glass and threw it at her, but of course it went straight through her and smashed on the floor.

Eventually, the other nurse came back and just laughed at my account of what had happened, telling me lots of stories about the Grey Lady's visits and how things would mysteriously go missing when she was around. Yes, her name in life had been Elizabeth (see Chapter Two). After I qualified and went back to this same hospital, she seemed to take a liking to me.

Another wonderful friend I made and knew for years was Greta, who was the Sister of a department I worked in and who was quirky, independent, adventurous and generous. She had never married although, she said, "I had my chances – a tribal chief, a Chinese surgeon and others." When she passed over she left her body to medical science, just the kind of thing she would do. She was 'old school' and would tell me tales of her nursing life working all over the world when we were on the same shift and I gave her a lift to work. It was a bit disconcerting that she prayed every time she got into my car… "Am I a bad driver?" I asked eventually.

"No," she said, "not you, it's all the other idiots. I pray to the angel who once saved my life.

"I was on a yacht in Italy owned by one of the surgeons I worked for," she went on. "There were six of us spending a week on the yacht, planning to sail around the Amalfi coast. One evening we were enjoying the champagne and dancing to the music, when suddenly we noticed that the engine had stopped and we were drifting out to sea. There was water coming in at the bottom of the yacht too. We assumed the captain must have stopped the engine so we all went down below and found the captain laid out dead on the floor. It was getting dark now and the water was rising.

"We were scared and some people were crying because none of us could swim and we were in the middle of the ocean. We didn't know what had happened to the captain and of course we didn't want to be blamed for his death. Well, we sobered up fast and someone said we should put out a May Day call, but the equipment wasn't working.

"Then we saw a shimmering light at the side of the boat. Some people thought it was a mermaid because it looked like she had seaweed in her hair in a sort of crown and she was floating at the side of the boat, but she had a flowing turquoise gown on. She looked straight at me with aquamarine eyes like little crystals and said, 'You are safe now. I am Asariel, angel of the sea.' Then she just vanished.

"A little while later, the boat began to move again but there was no sound from the engine. Then we heard a loud voice,

86

someone using a foghorn saying, 'We got your May Day message, we're coming to get you.' But none of us had sent a message because all the equipment had gone down." They were rescued and as they sat in the lifeboat the lifeguard told them that someone had made a distress call and given the name of the boat. When Greta told me this story, she still had unanswered questions about this mystery.

As part of my training I also had to work in a nursing home. The first day I walked in I saw all the chairs in a circle with the patients facing one another. It was heart-breaking to see these poor old folk, many with dementia, who had been through the war and brought up their families, just sitting staring at the floor perhaps going over memories in their minds but having no-one to share them with. I was only there to observe but I wanted to get stuck in and help the carers all I could.

There was a well-dressed man sitting by the window reading The Lord of the Rings – I thought heck, I could never finish that book, is he just pretending to read it? He said, "I bet you thought I was gaga, reading this. It's hard going but I am going to finish it." After lunch I went to find him in his room and he started to tell me his background.

"I was in the Army during the war. All my mates were blown to bits and I was the only survivor. I've carried this guilt all through my life." As he was speaking, a spirit woman appeared beside him, short and plump, wearing a green twinset with two rows of pearls. She stood smiling at the old chap, then she said, "That's my George, he was my hero." I didn't say anything because I didn't want the man to think I was a nutcase, so I kept quiet. However, she was having none of it, she actually poked my arm and said, "Tell him I'm here." So I just said, "Can you smell that lovely scent of Yardley April Violets?"

"You're going to think I'm crackers," he said, "but my late wife Mary always wore that perfume." He looked at me quizzically so I told him that, yes, Mary was standing beside him wearing a green twinset and two rows of pearls. "I knew it," he said. "She was a bossy old thing but she kept me going. Hello, love." She asked me to tell him she loved him and would be waiting at the Pearly Gates when his time came. Then two male spirits in army uniform came forward and one said, "He is a hero. Tell him that Tom and Harry are here and he's not to feel guilty." I relayed this message to George and his eyes filled with tears.

"We all came from the same district and knew each other as lads," he told me. "That's why they called us PALS – battalions of men who had enlisted together in local recruiting drives, with the promise that they would be able to serve alongside friends rather than being randomly allocated to different battalions.

"Well, we were stationed in France and five of us were sent on scouting duty looking for the enemy. We got to a small isolated farm and were just having a break when we heard trucks so we hid, hoping they'd go past. But they didn't. Women and children, some babes in arms, were dragged from the truck at gunpoint and lined up – it was clear the enemy were going to shoot them so we crept outside and shot the enemy soldiers. We loaded the women and children back onto the truck and took them to the barracks; we saved fifteen lives that day. Next day we were scouting again, just the four of us, Tom and Harry and Pete and me, and we found another isolated cottage and thought we'd have a break. Tom opened the door with Pete and Harry close by but it was booby-trapped – they must have known we were coming. My mates were blown to bits and I was the only survivor, and I had to leave them because I heard the enemy coming.

"I ran through the woods and got lost so I sheltered in a cave to catch my breath, when a voice said, 'Take the lower pathway, you will be safe.' It just came from nowhere and I thought I was going mad. But it felt like I was given new strength so I did go that way and found my way back to the barracks." He paused for a moment with a tear in his eye, and said quietly, "The guilt has never left me."

Later, George had gone into the first church he saw and asked aloud who had saved him. A priest had appeared from nowhere and told him it was God's will that he'd been saved. "All He asks is your daily prayers," said the priest so, ever since, George had prayed every day for forgiveness and given thanks for being saved. I reminded him that his mates had come through in spirit to say he was a hero; after all, they had themselves saved fifteen lives together so he should not feel guilty but proud of himself and his mates who gave their lives for others. George said he hadn't told anyone else this story except Mary, and now felt like a burden had been lifted from his shoulders.

The following day I found him sitting with his bag packed ready for his daughter to take him home. It seems that she and her family had been on holiday and George only came into the nursing home to give them a break. "I'm so glad I came, though," he said to me when she arrived, "because you've given me peace of mind after all these years." His daughter said, "I hope you haven't been telling the nurse naughty stories, Dad!" I told her that her father was a hero and now he had a wonderful story to tell her. George got up and hugged me.

"It was divine intervention that brought you here," he said to me, "and now I am going home – and Mary is coming with me." Six months later I read in the local paper that he had died, reunited with his beloved wife.

There was another old fellow there who actually was a bit gaga, walking up and down the room carrying a stick over his shoulder like a rifle because he thought he was still in the war in Belgium. The old ladies would shout at him, "Sit down, you silly old fool, the war's over," but he always replied that, for him, it wasn't. When I served his tea, he'd say, "Thank you, Florence Nightingale."

One day when we were alone he said, "I'm not as daft as they think I am, you know. The other nurses say I'm telling lies but not about the war I don't – I seen them with my own eyes." That pricked my interest so I asked him what he meant.

"I was in Belgium, at Mons, and the enemy had surrounded us. We were up to our eyes in mud and thought we were goners.

Suddenly we heard a noise and all looked up in the sky where there were these three really big angels. We'd been praying that help would come and it did, they saved our lives. It was a bloody miracle and it happened right before my eyes. The enemy retreated and we were safe." With that he stood up and began to march around the room singing God Save the Queen. The Angels of Mons is a famous story and here was a man who claimed to have been there.

In another nursing home I came across Harriet, who was very religious. No-one seemed to have time to talk to her but I loved to hear the old folk talk about their lives and what they'd done, and about their families. Harriet's relatives had moved her into the home because she had limited mobility and they thought she might fall over, and she was angry with her son for doing this because she'd loved her home. Still, her mind was as sharp as a razor.

When I served her afternoon tea she asked me if I would take her for a walk; there was a park nearby with lots of kiddies always playing in the water and on the swings and slides. I thought it was a great idea to get out into the fresh air and I said I'd get together some sandwiches and cake so we could have a picnic. Harriet gave me the most gorgeous smile. The manager noticed what was happening and said, "No-one else ever thinks to take patients out to the park. I'll get another nurse and two more patients to come with you." So we set out like a wagon train of wheelchairs and the patients were so happy because it was a beautiful day.

"Snowdrops remind me of angels," she told me. "I would like a few to put in a pot before I die – can you pick some for me?" There were no rules about picking flowers back then. I felt that she wanted to talk privately to me so we moved a little way from the others. "I know I'm dying," she said (yes, she did have cancer although no-one had told her), "because I've seen an angel. He had a book in his hand and said to me, 'This is the book of your life.'" I replied that this might have been Archangel Uriel and naturally Harriet asked me how I knew about angels, so I told her

90

about my Grandma Mac and how we used to pray to a different angel each day. She went quiet for a moment and then said, "Oh dear, I have to tell you something, I have to tell someone. I've been bad but my husband is dead and even he doesn't know what I'm telling you." I thought to myself, well, he will now!

"I had a baby out of wedlock," she went on. "The father was a married man so it all brought shame to my parents' door. I couldn't keep the baby and she was to be adopted and placed in a nursery at first with other babies who were going to be adopted. She had beautiful long black hair and I'd cut some off to save in a locket.

"I went to see her for the last time – I wasn't allowed to go inside and pick her up so I had to look through the glass. My heart was breaking. I had carried my little girl for nine months and now she was going to grow up not knowing her mother. I saw coloured lights around her cot and then a figure in a white dress appeared next to her cot. I assumed it was the nurse come to take her away. But then before my eyes the figure in white suddenly spread its wings, they were golden and they enclosed my little girl. Then it vanished and I slipped away quickly."

Harriet had tears running down her cheeks as she told me her sad story, but that wasn't the end of it. She wiped the tears and continued. Unmarried mothers were ostracised in those days and kept away from the other mothers and babies, and Harriet sat talking with some of them. Just then they heard screaming and saw a nurse running down the ward with a baby girl in her arms – it was Harriet's daughter and she had died. I put my arm around her and said, "The angels came for her, for whatever reason, and they will have looked after her."

"They knew how much I wanted to keep her," she smiled now, "and must have thought, well, if Harriet can't have her then no-one can." I thought she was looking peaky so we went back to the nursing home where I put her to bed and went to get her some tea. When I came back, I could smell the scent of white roses, the fragrance of Archangel Gabriel. Harriet grabbed my hand and asked, "Do you think I shall see my daughter again?" I told her that her daughter would be grown up now and would be waiting for her when she passed over. "That's good," she said, "because I'll soon be with her, nurse. When you went to fetch my tea, I saw a glimpse of a white dress and just one golden wing…"

I had a couple of days off and when I returned to work her bed was empty; she had passed over the same night after our last conversation. At least she was now with her daughter, and that made me happy.

Joan is an old friend of mine who told me about her earlier life when she had become depressed and lonely, before she met her husband. She had tried counselling and antidepressants but nothing helped her overcome the black cloud hanging over her and she was desperate for help. One day she'd been sitting in a waiting room and picked up a magazine that another patient had left there, and came across an article about Angelic Reiki healing. Joan's interest was piqued because, she told me, she had seen an angel when she was a little girl and confined to bed with an illness. She had been asleep and as she opened her eyes she saw a beautiful angel with long blonde hair sitting on the edge of her bed and smiling at her. The angel then leaned forward and touched her hand before vanishing. Within a day or two she felt really well again and was able to get up.

Now an article about Angelic Reiki healing had turned up, reminding her of her childhood experience, and it felt to her like the angels were telling her to look into this. She found a qualified lady and when they spoke there was an instant rapport between them. Sure enough, the first treatment – when the healer connected with the angels and asked for healing for Joan – proved to be the turning point in her life.

"I walked out of that place a more confident and happy woman, and I improved with each treatment. Naturally, my interest in angels and in healing grew too. Eventually the depression completely subsided. Then during the sixth session, something incredible happened. As I lay quietly under my healer's hands, I began to see swirling coloured lights… and gradually these formed into a radiant Being with golden wings and a green sheen to his gown. Because of all that I'd learned by now, I knew instantly that he was the great healer Archangel Raphael himself! I was just transfixed with awe.

"He leaned forward, touched me gently on the nose and spoke to me, 'I choose you to become a healer, to help others how you have been helped.' I decided there and then that I'd become a healer. Well, when the archangel of healing calls you don't ignore him, so I began training as an Angelic Reiki healer myself and soon my life was really happy. Using my work to help others and bring healing to the world changed everything, and it probably wouldn't have happened if Raphael had not stepped in."

Joan has an incredible aura around her and everyone she meets becomes her friend. Another friend, Kathy, told me her story just after she had lost her Dad. Kathy was very close to him and she still relives the events. They had been together when he suddenly started to get chest pains but didn't tell her how serious it was, then he collapsed and died in her arms. For months afterwards, she kept going over the event again and again in her mind, asking herself whether she should have seen the signs and done this or that.

Then one day she was feeling particularly upset and sobbing into her pillow, which was wet with tears, when there was a change of atmosphere in the room. There was silence, then she felt a 'whoosh' and two large wings enfolded her until she stopped sobbing. She said, "The presence seemed to crush me and hold me tight. I don't know if it was my Dad or an angel." I told Joan that it sounded like an angelic visit, probably sent by her Dad who wanted to give her a big hug and let her know he was around her. It may well have been Jophiel, the angel of beauty, since Joan is in the beauty business.

We have seen that angels bring comfort and reassurance, inspiration and warnings of danger, to all kinds of people in all walks of life and whether they are religious or not. Another friend, Lily, told me about the time she was nearly mugged.

"I was walking on a lonely path one early morning with my bag over my shoulder. There was quite a bit of money in it that I'd saved up. I was going to meet my friend and we were excited to be going into town on our own. Well, I was on the other side of the road from her and I saw her watching something behind me and looking maybe shocked, then I heard a voice in my head say, "Run!" so I ran across the road to my friend. Looking back, there were three men who looked drunk watching us but now they turned away. I've always believed it was my guardian angel who told me to run because if I hadn't I would have been mugged or assaulted."

One dear lady I met, ninety years-old, certainly had her own personal guardian. She had come into my department to have her stitches removed, having sustained a fractured femur, and as I got the equipment ready she asked me, "Have you done this before, nurse?" I reassured her that I'd done it many times and she replied, "Good, because my husband is watching you and he used to be a surgeon." I smiled to myself and thought 'I'd better make sure I do a good job, then.'

We chatted as I worked and she told me she'd been a nurse in a military hospital in India when the surgeon had taken a shine to her – he called her his sunflower – and they were married within two weeks despite the objections of his family. By now I had taken out twenty stitches with another twenty to go and I asked the lady if she felt all right. She replied, "Oh yes, I'm fine, and he says you're doing a good job." At this point I could smell curry, and when I had put her dressing on and gone to dispose of the sharps I saw an orb in the corner of the room; within it was a man's face, bearded and with one light brown eye and the other darker. He was smiling at me and nodding his head.

The lady was clearly intelligent and spiritually aware so I told her what I'd seen and she confirmed that all the details were correct. Her husband was indeed in the room with us, checking that she was being well cared for. The ward Sister spoke to me later and asked if the old lady was confused because she'd said her husband was there while I'd been taking out her stitches. "That's right, he was," I said, matter of fact. She rang back after a few hours, puzzled, saying she thought patients only claimed to see dead relatives when they were ready to pass over. I assured her that our loved ones are often nearby and can drop in at any time, and it doesn't always mean we're about to die. This lady just had her own permanent guardian angel.

"But what are we going to do about the smell of curry?" she asked. I told her not to worry, he wouldn't be haunting the ward.

8

A New Career

After thirty years of working as a hospital nurse, I had an accident and then illness that forced me to retire. Of course, I'd been meeting and communicating with angels and spirits all my life but I knew that, if I wanted to continue helping other people to know the truth of these things, then I needed to do a mediumship development course. This was a wonderful experience (described in my previous book).

Soon after qualifying, a young man came to see me not so much for a reading but for reassurance that he would be with his relatives when he eventually passed over. I told him honestly that no-one can be exactly sure what happens when we die, but I believed in a Heaven where our spirit relatives would meet us. Then the real reason for his visit emerged...

"My friend was electrocuted," he said, "very badly burnt and he died. I can't help thinking that he blames me." I was able to tell him that his friend was there with him, and I described his dark hair and eyes and that he came wearing a green jumper and carrying a scout's knife. The man started to sob. His spirit friend said it had just been an accident and he was not to blame himself; he was now waiting for his mate to roam the valleys like they used to do together. The young man then asked, "Does that mean I am going to die soon?" I reassured him that, no, he was just saying they would meet again in the afterlife and he went away happily.

But with another young man who came to see me it was a very different story altogether and as soon as he came into the room I could see that his aura was a horrible murky grey. I told him what the procedure was for the reading and asked if he was okay with Spirit perhaps coming through – some people fear the afterlife and spirit communication, so I always warn clients before I begin the reading – but he just looked vacant as though he didn't understand what I was saying. I offered him a choice of cards to choose from and he picked out the Angel Ascended Masters Witch Tarot. When I began the reading he was very still and didn't utter a word. The first four cards out told me, if I hadn't already realised, that this guy was in trouble so I asked him if there was anything he would like to know.

"Yes, there is," he said quietly and then paused for a moment. "I am a burglar. Am I going to prison?" The cards' answer to that was easy but then the spirit of his father appeared beside him and showed me prison bars, so I passed on the information. "I thought I'd got away with it," he muttered, "but thanks for that anyway. I'm prepared now."

The next card symbolised living abroad and his father con- firmed it, saying that the young man would be going back to Ireland. I told him that his father was with him and what he'd said, and for the first time the young man showed some emotion. He replied, "My Dad fell through a roof doing a burglary and I was with him. I am so sorry, Dad." Then the card of Forgiveness came into the reading and the father called out to his son to give himself up and pay the price, but that was a step too far for my client who promptly stood up and ran for the door shouting, "I will never give myself up!" With that he was gone. A few weeks later I read that he had been sent to prison for twelve months but I didn't know whether he'd taken any notice of what his father advised.

I felt sad for him but then nine months later there was a much happier sequel to the story. The young man came back to see me and apologised for the way he'd behaved. He was holding a baby! "She hadn't told me she was expecting until I was inside. I'm a reformed character now and I was let out early for good behaviour. I want to make her proud of me."

Early on in my new career I was asked by the owner of a garden centre to do a psychic demonstration event (because I had predicted something for them and it had come true). A buffet would be provided too and then I would give the demonstration. I was rather nervous because I had never done something like this in public before, so I asked my daughter to help and she gave me a session of hypnotherapy for confidence. I then did a meditation beforehand and asked – or begged – Spirit for help and to bring relatives forward for the people coming.

I needn't have worried. As soon as I started the demonstration I saw lights like little orbs in a row near the front; they were around a young woman whose spirit Mum came forward. She said, "Tell her I am here with our four cats and Mama cat has her babies with her. I died with liver cancer. Oh yes, and tell her I like her new boyfriend!" I approached the girl and passed on the message, which she confirmed was accurate. She went on, "When our cat died she was having kittens and she died with the kittens inside her. We think she was poisoned."

There then came one of those really awkward moments for a medium – and remember I was quite new to this way of doing things – when the young woman's mother gave me some very delicate information and a name. I had to make a quick decision and asked her daughter to stay behind after the event because I had a private message for her. She came up to me after the demonstration and I told her that her mother had given me the name of the person who poisoned their cat. Did she want me to tell her? She nodded so I passed on the information and she said, "Thank you. I was pretty sure it was her." Phew!

After that first message, a coloured orb began to circle the head of an elderly lady. She was wearing a beautiful angel pendant. This time there was a lady's face within the orb and I asked the lady if she would like to receive a message from her sister. She replied, "Well, that's what I've paid my money for." Right, I thought, this is going to be a tough one, but then the lady's sister came through clearly and she was wearing the same angel pendant.

"There are wonderful angels up here, Kath," she said. "Did you see the one that came for me?" The lady was flabbergasted, especially when I pointed out that she was wearing the same angel pendant as her sister – and her shoes! "Yes," she replied, "I put my sister's angel pendant round my neck before we buried her. And yes, I always loved those shoes." Everyone laughed and any nerves I might have had disappeared. Spirit never lets me down.

One of the most gratifying things about my work – apart from proving that we never die, of course – is the healing it can bring to those who are grieving. The lights were shining over a man's head now and I told him that I had his Dad here. "Oh my God," he said, "I wasn't expecting any message, I only came to keep my wife company." But Spirit always know who really needs their help.

I said that his Dad had seen him digging the garden with a fork when a robin had appeared nearby. "That was a sign from me," he said, "to let you know I'm Head Gardener here." His son explained that he and his father had worked together as gardeners but one day his Dad had chest pains and collapsed while digging. His son had tried CPR but it was too late and his father died in his arms. "He always called himself the Head Gardener and years ago he said that when he died he would send me a robin to let me know he was okay." The man was sobbing now so we took a break. He came to find me and said, "I don't know how these things happen. I've always felt guilty that I couldn't save him but I can move on with my life now."

The next spirit to come forward was a stocky little man wearing a uniform and with a feather in his hat, telling me that his daughter was here and she grew trees. That seemed very odd but I'd learned never to question what Spirit tells me. I relayed the message to the audience and a lady put her hand up. "Yes, that's my Dad," she said. "I grow Bonsai trees as a hobby. And he did have a feather in his hat, part of his uniform though I can't quite recall which regiment he was in." Then she said she had something to show me and took out a photo of her Dad in his uniform, complete with hat and feather in it. Everyone gasped – there could hardly be a better proof of spirit contact. I thanked her Dad for coming through to her and he replied, "It's my pleasure. I saw my chance so I took it."

The rest of the event went very well with several more spirits coming forward. I thanked them and my spirit guide for making it happen and a lot of people went home happy having heard from loved ones. My public demonstration baptism had been nothing to be nervous about after all, I had loved doing it and was asked to go back to do another one. For health reasons, though, I felt I had to take a step back from this kind of event and instead continued with private readings. These are normally one-to-one and I don't like to see couples because 'secret things' may emerge. But one couple were insistent and I thought it might be good to test myself...

As soon as they walked I could see that the man had an attitude; his aura was a bright orange, which usually signifies a very intelligent person, though it also had holes in it representing arrogance. On the other hand, the woman's aura was a royal blue with pink in it, usually suggesting that she was very much in love and a nice person. Still, it was obvious who was taking the lead for this reading. When I asked them if there was anything specific they wanted to know, he replied, "Yes, my mother has dementia and I want to know when she will die." Hmm, my instinct with seeing auras never lets me down.

I said, sorry, but I had no knowledge of when his mother would die. Actually, I could have told him exactly when she would pass over but I felt sad that this was all he had come for; in any case, it just isn't professional for a medium to give this sort of information so I kept quiet (and didn't tell him what I thought of him, either). Another thing I didn't tell him was that his father was standing beside me shaking his head. The woman then became overwhelmed, starting to cry, and I knew she was grieving for her Mum and would have loved the opportunity to bring her Mum forward. How could her husband be so insensitive, taking over the reading? And then it just happened, the woman's mother came through clearly.

"He has always been an arrogant b......," she said (yes, spirits do swear). "Go on, tell them I'm here." She seemed a proper matriarch and I bet she was the same when she was alive. I told the lady her Mum was here and wanted to know why they'd pulled up her African violet plants. She nearly fainted and said, "It wasn't me, it was him." Her husband shouted, "I didn't want reminding of the bitch – she scratched me!" and he showed me the marks on his arm. This was getting out of hand now so I told them we should end the reading, but he insisted, "I'll give you one hundred pounds if you tell me when my mother will die." I repeated that I couldn't do that. This story didn't end there, however, and it had more than one strange twist to it. The same lady rang me a year later.

"I thought you'd like to know this," she said. "One day soon after your reading I was sitting alone in a church and crying when I suddenly saw a beautiful vision of an angel and my Mum standing with her, both smiling. The angel had a green robe on and my mother was wearing the dress I buried her in. She spoke to me in my mind, 'I am here to help you with your sorrow.'" She went on to apologise for her husband being arrogant and selfish but said she had got through all that and her life had completely changed. Just before our reading, she had met another man who loved her (so that's why the pink was so bright in her aura, she was in love) but they'd only had six months together before he had a heart attack.

Her mother-in-law had in fact died a month after the reading and left her fortune to this woman's husband. But now he had also recently died, leaving all the money to the woman, who had met another man and was happy again... You couldn't make it up. Finally, she said she had a present for me and would drop it off: it turned out to be African violet plants, which are now thriving in my garden.

Whenever a client comes into my house they are protected by four archangels. I have always done a meditation beforehand to ask for their presence in the four corners of the room and thanked them for watching over us. They are Michael, the warrior carrying a laser sword, Raphael the healer, Uriel the protector and Gabriel, who cares for families. I burn Guardian Angel incense and usually begin a reading using angel cards. The special energies of crystals will be with us too: lapis lazuli, tiger's eye, rock quartz, Herkimer diamond and Faden quartz. Lastly I will have to hand my citrine pendulum, which I call Christine.

One lady who came to see me for a reading was very nervous and pregnant, her aura a pale blue edged with black. My intuition about this combination of colours was that she had lost someone quite young. She wanted me to talk through what we were going to do, so firstly I reassured her about her safety by describing my preparations.

"I am an older mother, so they used to tell me at the clinic. I have lost four babies in the past five years, all at seven months old, so I'm terrified I will lose this baby too. I can't feel it kicking." I asked her if she would kindly let me put my hand on her belly and when I gently laid my hand there I could feel the energy flowing through me. All of a sudden there was an enormous kick! "Oh my God," she said, "what did you do?" I told her it was just a coincidence and of course didn't mention that I'd been worried when she came in. Her baby was well now, anyway, and nearly ready to meet his Mum – though hopefully not today. Next, she wanted to know what the sex was and I suggested we do a card reading.

But just as we began the reading, her Nana came through and said, "It's a boy, a big healthy boy. Please tell her I'm here and thank her for the teddy bear she put in my coffin." The lady was shocked. She told me that her grandparents had been in a car accident and had both died; she had been grieving for them for years. Then Nana came back in saying, "That's why she keeps losing babies, but this one is safe."

"Yes, that's true," said the lady. "I get distraught and don't look after myself, not on purpose, I just go into a mood." Grief can be a terrible thing for many people and it can ruin someone's life. But now she knew that her Nana would be with her when she had her boy (she said that all the babies she'd lost were girls). We decided to see what the cards would say anyway.

Archangel Jeremiel	All is well. Everything is happening exactly as it should – and with hidden blessings, as you will soon see.
Archangel Sandalphon	Gifts from God. The angels are looking after your babies in Heaven. Open yourself now to receive the gifts the Creator has granted you.
Archangel Zadkiel	Your prayers have been heard and answered. Have faith, all will be revealed very soon. A big surprise is coming very shortly.
Archangel Gabriel	Your loved ones in Heaven are doing well and send you greetings. Let go of your worries and feel their loving blessings around you.
Archangel Azrael	I am with you in your time of need, helping your heart to heal.

She was very happy with the card reading although, to be honest, I was curious to know more because I felt there was something else going on with his lady but couldn't put my finger on it. So I asked her if she would like me to use my pendulum to check on the baby's sex. "I ask my guide, Black Feather, questions and he answers," I explained. "If the pendulum moves from left to right that means 'No' and if it spins it's a 'Yes'." I asked whether the baby was a boy and watched with bated breath as the pendulum swung from side to side and then started to spin... I knew immediately what was happening here: she was having two babies!

She clearly didn't know this and it wasn't my place to enlighten her either. Instead, I said, "I need you to go to the doctor's now. No, there's nothing wrong with the baby but I think you need extra care, what with losing your Nana and Grandad and all that's happened." Her reply really surprised me: she didn't trust doctors, hadn't seen one at all during her pregnancy and had decided simply to have the baby at home. Having moved here from the south, she hadn't even registered with a local doctor. I just said, "Well, you won't be having this baby at home, trust me. Please go and see a doctor. After all, you came to see me because you were worried that the baby might not be well." Finally she agreed and I breathed a large, silent sigh of relief.

A little while later she came back. "You knew, didn't you? I'm having twins." I nodded and smiled. It would be a boy and a girl, according to the pendulum, and four weeks later she brought them to see me. The angel cards had promised 'hidden blessings' and 'a big surprise' – it was certainly that.

I have had a lot of pregnant ladies coming to see me and wanting to know the sex of the child but I can't always help them. Sometimes I am given the sex of the baby and other times there's nothing, for whatever reason. All the same, these readings, like the last one, are usually happy and successful. But not so with one particular lady, a regular client, who wanted to ask if her baby was her husband's or her lover's! I knew straight away but I didn't feel it would be professional to go into that sort of personal issue.

However, the lady's Mum then came through strongly and just said one word, a man's name. "Oh no, that's my boyfriend," my client said. "And tell Mum she can sod off!" Well, the mother had been determined to come through and speak to her daughter, although she was angry and a lot of it was very personal, with a few insults thrown in for good measure too. It wasn't one of the nicest readings I've done but Mum would not go away; sometimes spirits just want to say what they felt they never could when alive on Earth!

Many of my angel card readings have pulled at the heart-strings. Tina phoned me desperate for a reading, so I told her to come later that day and in due course she walked, or rather wobbled, in obviously intoxicated. She told me she was an alcoholic and asked if I was still willing to go ahead; well, I don't pass judgement, my job is to help people. She told me that she kept 'seeing things' and wanted me to help her understand why – perhaps she was ill? I have quite a selection of Tarot cards and she chose Angel and Goddess cards. With each one, I began the reading with my intuition taking over and bit by bit she told me her story.

The Angel of Guidance

I could see that Tina had been feeling a bit confused lately, unsure which direction to take, and I reassured her that the angels would guide her. "But how do I find them?" she asked. I said that they would find her, she just needed to have faith and open her heart. "I didn't come here for a sermon," she said. This was not going to be easy.

The Angel of Addiction and Healing

As soon as this card came out Tina started to cry. She had been, she said, living the good life with expensive cars, jewellery, exotic holidays and a husband who adored her, but foolishly had a secret affair with a younger man. One evening, having been with her lover, she came home to find that her husband had suffered a

106

heart attack and died. That's when she started drinking. Her lover went away, her husband left her nothing in his Will and at his funeral his daughter had publicly shamed her.

The Angel of New Life

I could see now that a new chapter was ready to unfold for her, with a sense of clarity and purpose and… good heavens, she would discover a gift for clairvoyance. She didn't seem too surprised by this. "I am always seeing things and I seem to know things," she said. "I can feel my husband around and I'm scared he's haunting me."

Spirit now took over and her husband came into view, showing me his gold front tooth and gold-rimmed glasses and saying that he had forgiven her. Tina asked if she could talk to him and told him that she loved him and been stupid to do what she did because now her heart was breaking. My large lapis lazuli crystal with gold flecks then rolled over on its own and nearly fell onto the floor. That was his acknowledgement of her.

The Angel of Self Worth

"You are undervaluing yourself," I told her, "and you can be so much more. When you came in, your aura was red and brown with anger but now it's changed to pink and green, healing colours."

"And I can see yours," she smiled. "It's purple and silver. I feel different now that my husband has forgiven me." Tina needed to love herself again and then others would be able to love her too, so I suggested this mantra (using a pink candle):

> *I am a being of light and love.*
> *From this moment I will honour and value myself.*
> *I am worthy of everyone's love.*
> *I thank the angels for guiding me.*

The Goddess of the Sacred Pathway

"Let go of logic and trust your feelings," I said. "Your life will change so keep a journal of what happens and you'll look back in twelve months' time and see that you've been led down a new sacred pathway." She gave me a hug and I felt all the negativity leave her body.

The Goddess of Knowledge

It was time for Tina to start putting into practice what she already knew and to trust her intuition in sorting her life out. First, she needed help for her alcohol problem, of course, and then she should join a mediumship development course to understand better what was happening. The goddess of knowledge, Athena, would guide her (helped, incidentally, by purple and blue crystals such as amethyst and lapis lazuli, along with black tourmaline for grounding, turquoise for protection and green aventurine for healing).

Goddess of Strength

Tina was going to need inner strength to develop her spiritual work and break longstanding patterns of behaviour. She said, "I know – and I know that I've been given a second chance. But I feel so much lighter and more confident already." She promised to deal with her alcoholism and look for a mediumship development course. Then she seemed to become fascinated by the crystals on my table and asked what the significance of the rose quartz was.

"It represents love," I told her. "A new man will come into your life next year." She brought him to meet me twelve months later, they had met on a retreat and were clearly soulmates. And she was very different, softer yet confident. She had developed her clairvoyance too and moved abroad where she teaches about spirituality together with her new chap.

The most troubled and challenging life can be turned around!

What happens when we die? What do we experience and where do we go? These are the questions I am asked most often and indeed I often wonder about them myself. Along with other mediums, I receive spirit accounts yet there are so many different descriptions and nobody can be absolutely sure of 'the truth' (if there is one truth). I count myself very fortunate to have the spiritual gifts that enable me to talk to spirits from the other side of life, yet most of those who come through are more concerned about identifying themselves to the relatives and friends they have left behind than saying what Heaven is like.

In recent years there has been a lot of research into the Near-Death Experience (NDE) and perhaps this provides evidence of what people go through when they pass over. In fact, a lot of spiritual teachers have claimed that the NDE finally gives us proof of the afterlife.

Most of the research has involved patients who have suffered a cardiac arrest and been treated in hospital. Some of those who survive then say that in fact they were conscious throughout their operation and went on a strange spiritual journey to the very edge of life. The classic account that has received most public attention is that this journey involves passing through 'a tunnel of light' that gets brighter and brighter until the end of the tunnel is reached; some have said that they were encouraged along this tunnel by spiritual beings.

When they emerged, there was a great feeling of peace and freedom from all pain, perhaps finding themselves in a beautiful garden with vivid colours. But then there would be some kind of barrier or gateway, symbolising the end of the living journey; the person knows that if they cross that barrier they will not return to earthly life. On the other side of the barrier they might see deceased relatives or 'Beings of light', angelic figures surrounded by a mellow but not blinding light. (These descriptions vary according to the person's religious beliefs). In every case, the person is told that it is not their time to pass over yet, perhaps because they 'still have work to do' on Earth. The person then simply floats back into their physical body and comes back to normal consciousness in the hospital.

When these people tell their stories later they say that they knew they were on the edge of death and now have a new spiritual outlook. They appreciate better what's really important in this life and have become 'better people', even changing their whole way of life. The NDE does seem, then, to offer the best insights we have about what dying feels like and how the spirit world appears.

However, if we dig a bit deeper into the published research, we find that the story is not always so clear and, in fact, the NDE experience is not always so pleasant. Without going into too many figures, it turns out that only about one in six NDE accounts involve the tunnel of light and less than one in ten include that beautiful landscape or welcoming relatives. About a quarter of these patients actually describe a rather frightening experience, and the after-effects are not always so spiritually enlightening.

And it's not just cardiac arrest patients who tell us about NDEs. They can also occur during other kinds of trauma or even deep meditation, making it very difficult for doctors to understand exactly what is happening in the body. One thing that is clear, though, is that our consciousness is not just housed in our brains since life goes on for quite a time when the brain shows little or no electrical activity. There are many theories about what is really happening during a NDE – such as chemical substances causing a kind of dream state – and the jury is still out. We cannot say for sure that we now have proof of a life after death since, after all, the people who have had this experience didn't die!

Now, the actual ending of a life is a very special moment. Sometimes, sadly, it is traumatic. But in very many other cases, relatives and holy men and those who care for sick patients such as doctors and nurses, tell of a different kind of deathbed experience.

As I have described in this book (and my earlier one) there may be a peaceful energy felt in the room, the sense of another presence and the vision of the person's aura changing. I am certainly not the only one to have witnessed spirit relatives, doctors or angels caring for the patient and keeping them safe, then seeing the soul separate from the body as the silver cord breaks and they leave the Earth on their journey to another world. And so many spirit communicators have come back to my clients to say that there is nothing to fear.

So we cannot be sure of the answer to that question, 'What happens when we die?', and perhaps it is different for different people anyway. But the Near-Death Experience is certainly fascinating and can have a profound effect on someone. My friend Mary gave me her first-hand account. She was only fourteen years-old when she became breathless and was coughing so much that she nearly choked to death.

"It was in May when I became critically ill. It had started out a normal day, but things changed in a heartbeat. I became breathless and coughing, I couldn't speak and then it got worse and I went into kidney and lung failure. In a side ward at the hospital, I thought I was going to die, trying not to fall asleep, yet I felt a calmness come over me. At the same time I felt really guilty for the people who loved me and I was leaving behind – my parents were distraught, so much so that my mother could not be in the same room as me because she felt completely helpless. Well, I made it through the night and the following morning I was taken to Theatre for a lung and kidney biopsy, then put on a ventilator in Intensive Care. No-one expected me to pull through and apparently I was given the Last Rites.

"Even though I was unconscious, what I could sense was a guardian angel nearby; the angel was tall and very beautiful, making me feel safe and loved. Then I saw a tunnel with different people walking through it, everyday normal people like businessmen in suits with briefcases, mums with pushchairs, people walking their dogs… Next thing I remember was finding myself in a stunningly beautiful garden where the grass was an amazing green and the hedges were neatly cut, and I was walking along a path around a square. The sky was an amazing blue too and the temperature was ideal, not too hot nor cold. Up in the distance I could see people going through a gate at the top of a field, children and other people running up to the gate, but somehow I knew I wasn't allowed up there. Then I was then sent back through the tunnel.

"When I regained consciousness, I was taken to a High Dependency ward in the hospital because I was still critical and no-one could say if I would survive. I felt extremely exhausted, my father was fast asleep in a chair but I couldn't sleep; I noticed the wall clock showing 1 a.m. exactly. Suddenly I felt someone touch my hand filling me with so much energy and I was hardly expecting what happened next – my body was being lifted up and I crashed out of the hospital roof, spinning around with great power. It was so beautiful, I cannot really describe it but I felt elated. A voice said, 'It is not your time yet, you have something important to do on Earth. Do not fear death.' I felt a presence beside me and when I looked round I saw an angel.

"From that moment on I began to be aware of my spirit family and my spirit guides. I've had several operations since then and often see my room filled with spirits when I wake up from an operation, they are always there to greet me. It's cool! When my Grandma passed over after a serious illness a few years later, I felt relief for her; of course, I loved and missed her but it gave me great comfort to know she is in Spirit. Having glimpsed the Other Side, I knew she was safe and back home at last.

"Even when I thought I was leaving my family myself, I felt no grief or sadness. Some people might think that's an awful thing to say, but to me it's as though there's no need for grief as we experience it on Earth; it just isn't like that in Spirit, it doesn't exist. You'd imagine that, as a mother of three children, death would be unthinkable, the ultimate devastation, but in reality there's no separation, we are all one, never apart and all connected. I genuinely don't think death is the end of anything, in fact I tell my children that life is an illusion.

"After I was well, for a while I wanted to 'go back home' and kept asking why I had to come back here, and what was the 'something important' I had to do on Earth? It became an obsession that my family couldn't understand. But then I worked hard to connect with Spirit, my guide came forward and now I give psychic readings. The other important thing that the NDE did was make me realise that so many things that people care about don't really matter, I mean the day to day things like cars, money, status. What's the point? We are always playing a game on Earth, far too seriously."

Mary's extraordinary experience, a view of 'paradise', was a once-in-a-lifetime event to be remembered forever and it gives us all another insight into the spirit world. I too have stepped into that world with its limitless vivid colours and now I am able to help spirit people come back to talk through me and bring messages for their loved ones. They are with us all the time – I couldn't count the number of times they have asked relatives to 'lay a place for me at Christmas'. Whatever the truth is about NDEs, we can be assured that there is life after death.

9

The Spirit of Animals

Angelic help is given with unconditional love to all in need, including animals, and sometimes the angels work through animals too – the archangels Fhelyai and Jeremiel in particular.

Many years ago, a lady told me that her family had a beautiful long garden with a large pond; this was decorated with a stone angel sculpture and, at the top, a rainbow that the owner had painted herself. Her two little girls were very mischievous and one day they decided to climb up the sculpture to touch the rainbow. The older one, who was four years-old, slipped and fell into the pond face down banging her head which started bleeding profusely. Her sister started to scream and tried to help but couldn't move her.

The family dog had been lying outside near the house enjoying the sunshine, being old, arthritic and deaf. Suddenly, according to the girls' mother who was looking out of a window, he was up on his feet and shooting down the garden with sparks of colour on his back, yellow, green, pink and purple. He dashed into the pond and grabbed the little girl's dress in his teeth, managing to turn her over. "It was like watching a slow motion film," said the lady. "I couldn't move and I was shocked by how quickly he moved and the beautiful colours that followed him."

Her daughter was admitted to hospital with a fractured skull but slowly got better. Later, her Mum asked her why she had climbed up the sculpture when she knew it was forbidden. She replied sheepishly, "That's what the angel said to me too." Seeing the disbelieving look on her Mum's face, she went on, "The angel really did speak to me. She said 'You are naughty climbing up me' and I was so surprised that's why I fell into the water."

Of course, I asked the lady how her old, deaf dog could have known that the girl was in trouble and she replied, "I have no explanation, he rarely moves." After the girl had come home, her mother decided to fill in the pond and plant it with flowers as a way of saying 'Thank you' to the angel; they particularly chose yellow, pink and purple pansies, the colours that had surrounded the dog when he made his rescue. After they had finished the work, they went back inside the house and found a white feather in the dog's bed.

My own daughter Karen had always owned a horse from when she was a girl. Charly died at twenty-five years-old and Karen decided to take a break from riding and train as an Angelic Reiki healer and as a hypnotherapist. Soon she longed for another horse though. She had always favoured chestnut horses but I had a dream of a white horse coming on a ferry boat from Ireland and to our family. I asked his name but couldn't get an answer, I just knew he was the right one for my daughter. When I told her about the dream she dismissed it, saying she would never have a white horse, but I was sure; Spirit would not have shown him to me if it meant nothing. She just smiled and walked away saying, "Yeah, Mama, you know best."

She saw a chestnut horse advertised in a magazine and she travelled quite a long way with her husband to the stables to see him. He was indeed lovely – but just then she heard a whinny and turned around to see a white horse looking straight at her in the eye as though to say, "It's me you want." She could hardly believe this was happening but when she went over to his stable he nuzzled into her neck and it was love at first sight; they were besotted with one another. He didn't have a name, he had just come over from Ireland on the ferry and only had the passport. That night I dreamed about him and heard the name Gabriel spoken. I didn't tell Karen this but suggested we each write down a name on paper and then compare them: we had both written 'Gabriel' so that's what he was called.

Karen and Gabriel have a deep spiritual connection. The people at the stables laugh when Karen is driving up the lane because Gabriel runs to the fence and starts whinnying as if to say, "Mum is here!" Did fate bring them together? Sometimes, no matter how hard we try to avoid something it still happens as if it's meant to. Gabriel proved to be quite a handful, he was stubborn, anxious and fearful at first because he'd had a traumatic time before, passed around to various unloving owners. But now Karen was able to give him Angelic Reiki healing; when she does this, he lays his head on her shoulder, falling asleep, and he has become peaceful and confident.[3]

I am a great animal lover myself and seem to have got a bit of a reputation for finding lost animals. A famer's wife once came to see me having travelled fifty miles; she was a no-nonsense kind of lady, the kind I would not generally expect to have faith in what I do. But she had seen me give a psychic demonstration in the past and thought I was 'real'. Her two border collies (sheepdogs) had been stolen and she asked if I could help her find them.

It's always tough when an animal's owner is naturally upset and expecting an answer straight away, so I sometimes do a card reading to take the pressure off me while I try to get information from Spirit. After a few minutes I was shown a dog lying

---

[3] Angelic Reiki healing attunements are not done by the teacher and the energy does not come through the teacher. Each individual is linked to their own angel who works through them to give healing. In meditation, the student is taken to the temple of the angelic 'kingdom of light' where there are thirty archangels, known as 'the Mighty Sarim'.

underneath a green plastic sheet with coloured orbs dancing along the top of it. (I believe the orbs were angelic beings keeping the dog alive until he could be found.) The other dog was chained up to a wall nearby. I told the lady that what I was seeing was quite graphic and asked if she was sure she wanted me to continue as the news might be bad. She replied, "Of course! I've had four husbands, buried two, and had six children so I'm not frightened by what you're going to tell me." We understood one another and created a bond that has lasted many years.

"I see both dogs in a barn," I told her. "One is chained up to the wall, the other has a green plastic sheet over it. On top of the sheet are coloured lights known as orbs, which means there is a spirit presence with the dog. The dog is not yet dead because I don't feel his spirit around me, but he's close." She told me that one dog was male, the other female, and they were worth thousands of pounds each because they were show dogs that had won prizes at sheepdog trials. "Money doesn't come into it as far as you're concerned," I said, "because you love these dogs with all your heart." She smiled and told me that she had four more dogs at home but these were her favourites.

"There's another vision now," I went on. "I am shown a man with ginger hair and a beard, wearing a black hat, and well-built." She gasped and said, "Oh no, not him!" Then I was shown the coloured logo and the name of a particular farm. The man went into the barn carrying a large syringe in his hand, lifted up the sheet and started feeding the dog through a muzzle while the female dog growled and barked at him. That was enough for the lady who said, "I know who that is. The farm is forty miles away from ours and he's a sheepdog breeder. Right, I'm phoning the police and my husband now."

She phoned me that evening to tell me that she had her dogs back and to thank me. (I did wonder what she told the police about how she knew where the dogs were!) "How did you know these things?" she asked. I replied that I am just a channel for Spirit, who tell me and show me what I need to know so I can pass it on. About a year after this she wrote to say that both dogs had again been in the trials, then Belle had had six puppies and Max was the dad. She also offered me one of the pups as a gift – they were worth a lot of money – but I had to say 'No' because I already had four dogs of my own. She later told me that she had called the pup Glyn after me!

When Spirit want me to know something they give me various visions, numbers or sounds when I'm meditating. For a while, I kept getting the name Rupert though I had no idea what it meant and definitely didn't know anyone of that name. All was to be revealed by my next client…

"Someone opened my parrot's cage and he has flown away," he told me. "He's very important to me so can you help find him?" I could see that the man's aura was dark green edged with grey, so I suspected there was a different kind of problem here. Anyway, I was given a vision of the woman who was responsible; she had him with another parrot and other birds. I never thought to ask the parrot's name but then the vision continued and I said, "He is with a lady who thinks he is hers. I'm being given the name Mabel."

"That's my ex-girlfriend's parrot!" he replied, getting a bit agitated. But then he became breathless and pulled out an inhaler. A spirit man appeared beside him and a voice in my head said, "Parrot disease." I had heard about that (psittacosis is a lung infection) from my time as a nurse on a chest unit, so now I said to my client, "I have your father here and he says you breed parrots. Dad is asking you to go to the doctor about your breathing as soon as you can. You have an illness connected to parrots that's causing your breathing problems. You really need to see a doctor."

"Good grief!" he said. "I only came to see if you could find Rupert." Off he went to get Rupert back from his ex-girlfriend – it turned out that she wanted to mate Rupert with Mabel – but that was not the end of the story and he came back to see me a month later. He hadn't gone to see a doctor because he thought they would make him get rid of Rupert. Then quite soon he began to feel poorly, his breathing became very difficult and he collapsed; but because he lived on his own, no-one knew and the man's condition was getting serious. Then Rupert saved the day! He started squawking, "Help, help, help!" until a neighbour heard him and called for an ambulance.

Rupert then had to go back to Mabel after all until his owner was well enough to go home. Having learned a lesson, he bought Rupert a new double cage so that Mabel and his girlfriend (no longer an ex-) could come and visit. "I am so careful cleaning out Rupert's cage now," he said. "If it hadn't been for you helping me get him back and then him squawking like that, I could have died."

Like the story of Rupert, some of my animal experiences have a real 'twist in the tail'! A lady came to see me because her cat had gone missing, and I saw by her aura, which was dark blue with pink dots, that she really loved the cat and was grieving. It was a beautiful Persian and had been missing for two weeks and no-one in the area had seen her. "She is a house cat," said the lady, "and only ever goes out at night for a short time. She doesn't even have a collar because she always comes home." Nothing was coming through to me yet so I knew the cat was alive; perhaps someone finding her had decided to keep her.

We decided to do a reading and during this I began to see a pink glow that looked like it had a cat's face in it. Whenever the colour pink comes into a reading, all is well – it often also means there's a pregnancy – so I knew then that wherever the cat was she was being looked after. I was then shown the cat herself, who had made a nest in a bale of hay where she had four little kittens! "That's not our Cleo," said the lady. "She's been splayed so she can't have kittens. You've got it wrong." I assured her that Spirit were giving me a clear message: the cat matched the lady's description, she had four kittens and was being looked after by the farmer's wife at a farm nearby.

My client rang back the next day to apologise for being abrupt and not believing me. It turned out that her husband had not taken Cleo to the vet to be splayed after all and she had mated with a ginger tomcat. "Now I have four beautiful kittens," she said. "There's three boys and a girl – would you like to name them?" The names Tinker, Tailor, Soldier and Sailor popped into my head; the lady laughed and said she loved those names, though the spelling of the girl's name was changed to Taylor!

Whitby is my favourite place. My husband Frank and I have had a caravan there for over twenty years and we just love to sit on the bench outside Saint Mary's church near the abbey and watch the world go by. I often go into the church to light a candle for those who have passed over – well, I use up a row of candles but always leave money for the church funds. It is a real pleasure to feel the beautiful atmosphere in this old church; there are small boxes where families used to sit together in past times, and I like to sit there to admire the church and take in its aura.

One day, though, I found myself involved in a really sad story. Inside the church there's a 'message tree' on which people pin personal notes for the vicar to read at a Sunday service. I noticed an elderly lady writing rather a lot of messages there and she looked across at me with tears streaming down her face. "I have no-one left," she said, and showed me the messages. They were in memory of Daisy, Snowdrop, Jade and Basil; I knew immediately that these were dogs because there were little spirit Yorkshire terriers playing around her feet. I said I was sorry for her loss and she studied me for a moment, then said, "I need to know where dogs go when they die. You know, don't you? Do you have time to sit with me and tell me about it, please?" I nipped outside to tell Frank I was going to be a while.

The lady got out her hanky and began to tell me her story. Her husband and daughter had died five years ago in a car accident. Being lonely, after a while she had adopted two little Yorkshire terriers, Daisy and Basil, and was told that Daisy had been splayed so she couldn't have puppies… you've guessed it, around eight weeks later the lady heard Daisy starting to squeal and watched her give birth to four puppies. Now she had six little Yorkshire terriers and was beginning to feel happier again. She called the pups Violet, Flora, Snowdrop and Jade. But four of her new family had now died, leaving only Violet, named after her sister, and Flora, named after the lady herself.

"I got a new next door neighbour," she told me, "a strange man who lived on his own, he was filthy and obese. I found out later that he was one of those people who have a mental illness but they said he was fit to live in the community. I tried to be friendly with him but he just shouted at me to keep the dogs quiet or I'd 'regret it'. Perhaps I should have told the police or someone, but I didn't want to make a fuss. I'm in my seventies and I just want a quiet life." She started to cry again so I put my arm around her until she felt ready to go on.

The dogs had all been in the garden, playing and yapping at each other as they do, when the neighbour had put his head over the fence and said, "Right, I warned you to keep them quiet. That's it!" The lady brought them all back inside but, while she was chatting on the phone, four of them had jumped out of a window leaving only Violet and Flora inside on their beds. She did call the police this time to ask for help but didn't mention her neighbour because she'd seen him go out in his car. In the evening there was a noise from her letterbox and four dog collars were lying on the carpet. Flora's other neighbour heard her scream and came rushing in. They found the little dogs in a sack in her dustbin. They had been drowned.

The police did interview the man and he admitted doing it, but the police said they couldn't do anything because he was mentally ill; instead, he was taken back to hospital where he now had to stay. But Flora had understandably been devastated and moved into a retirement home as she couldn't face living there anymore. At least she was able to take the remaining two dogs there with her.

Well, I don't go around randomly giving people messages from Spirit but I thought to myself that I had to use my gift here to help Flora. I said to her, "That is such an awful story, and thank you for telling me. Now I have something to tell you. I have lost many pets too so I know how you feel – my children had every pet you could imagine and my sister even had a white rat. I do know something about what happens when they die. Do you believe in an afterlife, because I don't want to upset you if you don't?" She said that she would love to hear what I had to say, and I breathed a silent sigh of relief.

"When you were writing those notes," I told her, "I saw a man beside you wearing a brown checked shirt and a green waistcoat. There was a lady with him wearing a yellow sun dress and she was holding a sunflower. Beside them were four little Yorkshire terriers, all shoving each other and trying to climb up your husband's legs. They're still here and he has his arms stretched out wide and says, 'Talk to me, Flo, when you put the kettle on.' And your daughter says she brought the sunflower for you."

Flora smiled for the first time since we'd met. "Ron loved his cup of tea. It was his mantra, 'Put the kettle on.' And yes, my daughter did bring me a sunflower and I have pressed it in my Bible." I thought to myself that when I'd come into the church to light candles I never expected to meet this lovely elderly lady with such a tragic story to tell. Yet, thank heavens, I am able to bring some comfort to those who are grieving.

There was some more. I asked her to look across to a nearby chair where there were four little lights dancing about, orbs in which we could clearly see eyes. These were her four dogs come back to see her. "When our pets die," I told her, "they go to a place called the Rainbow Bridge where they are met by Archangel Ariel and Saint Francis of Assisi who decide where the animals should be in the celestial realms. If they are ill or hurt, they are nursed back to health." Flora took my hand and kissed it, saying she could now go on with her life knowing that her babies were safe with Ron and her daughter.

We went outside the church where Frank was still sitting with our two dogs, watching the world go by, and Flora waved goodbye as she went off home. A week later, I went there to light candles again and thought I would just leave a message for her in case she came back, but she had already left one for me: 'Once in a while you come across a miracle. You brought mine.' Then around a year later when I entered the church I saw her sitting with her little red beret on facing the altar; I walked towards her to say 'Hello' – and she vanished. So now I light another candle whenever I go into that church.

10

Bringing The Angels Closer

What are the signs that angels give to show that they are close? You don't necessarily have to be a very spiritual person, or even believe in angels, but many, many people have seen the evidence and realised that there is something special about their experience.

One of the most common signs is a white feather appearing in an unusual place and at a significant time. Of course, there are those who say, "It's just a bird's feather." For me, there is a real difference because angel feathers are a brilliant white, fluffy at the bottom and with an alignment of straight feathers further up; they are also smaller than other birds' feathers which are layered. Still, it's the timing and location of an angel feather, or other special sign, that's really important and makes us know that we are being listened to and cared for – that we are not alone. For example, you may be very troubled or upset by something that's happened and decide to go out for a walk; there are no birds around at all, and yet a small fluffy white feather drifts down apparently out of nowhere right in front of you. Perhaps you decide to go into the garden, or to a park, a sit for a while on a favourite bench; when you get there, there is one small white feather waiting for you.[4]

Angels also seem to love the glitter of silver and gold. When I make a special request to the angels for someone who is ill or dying, to help them through their difficulty or accompany them on their last journey, I ask for some acknowledgement that they have heard me. Within a short time I will then find a small silver coin, for example, in an unusual place. (I keep these in my prayer box and put them in a charity box later).

Other silver items that turn up unexpectedly are pins. In my spare time, I make dolls and I am always extremely careful with pins and needles because I have two dogs and don't want them treading on them; but they turn up in unusual places such as in the sink or stuck in a chair. I have mentioned earlier that when my Mam was dying, I read her a story about Archangel Anael who wears a silver pin; I went into another room for a quiet moment, a room that was never used, and there was a silver pin on the floor. Mam never used pins. I went back to finish her story and she died a few hours later.

It's a similar story with odd coloured buttons. I always use run of the mill coloured buttons when making my dolls so I can distinguish between one of mine or an angel's. I have found theirs in the dogs' beds and in a teacup in the past and it's my belief that the colour defines the angel who has left it. I once asked for some healing for a certain lady who was very ill and she rang me later to say that she'd found a yellow button on her saucer that definitely hadn't been there before... did I know why? Well, I had included her in my prayers to Archangel Jophiel, the arch-angel of the yellow ray. She also said she was feeling a lot better now. When I was very ill myself a few years ago, I kept finding green buttons in unusual places and I could feel the presence of Archangel Raphael, the master healer.

---

[4] Editor's note: While working on this book at a computer next to a window that looked out onto a garden, a white feather drifted slowly down the glass.

A lot of people also say that they see special signs in the shapes of the clouds in the sky. Perhaps they look like angel wings or a face you recognise, even the shape of a much loved pet animal who has passed over. I often ask for angelic guidance when I am out walking and the clouds have helped me many times. Who knows how these shapes are made? It's an example of 'synchronicity', a special and meaningful sign that appears at a significant moment.

Another way that reassurance might come just when you need it is actually in words. I don't mean hearing a voice in your head (although that does work for some people) but happening upon a particular word or phrase that answers your prayer just after you have made it. It could be that you pick up a newspaper or book and open it at random, or turn on the radio just as a special song is playing, or you overhear a snatch of someone else's conversation at another table in a café. The words you read or hear will be an answer to your question or reassurance that angelic help is near.

Fragrances can help us become closer to the angels and I've even found that flowers can turn up in unusual circumstances. In particular, I know an angel is near when I smell the fragrance of white roses, which seems to be a favourite of theirs. We can use fragrances to invoke individual angels and draw them closer to help us with particular issues.

Archangel Raphael	He is the master healer and is drawn to us using sandalwood, neroli and juniper (especially good when used for a massage).
Archangel Zadkiel	Focus on the spiritual centre at your crown and ask Zadkiel to bring wisdom, knowledge and understanding by using frankincense, rosemary and sage. Zadkiel also helps to cleanse our auras, with eucalyptus, lemon and juniper.

Archangel Tzaphkiel	Invite Tzaphkiel of the violet ray to help you meet your guides and angels during your meditation, using violet, clary sage and lavender.
Archangel Gabriel	The angel of dreams will come into your consciousness while you sleep, bringing colours, visions and messages of guidance. Prepare with mimosa, spearmint, coriander and sage.
Archangel Raziel	Raziel brings us to a higher level of guidance and divination through visions and other spiritual experiences. We can connect with myrrh, sandalwood and cinnamon.
Archangel Uriel	He also enhances our visions and helps us to reach out to the angelic realms. Use jasmine, lemon, verbena and rose otto.
Archangel Chamuel	Chamuel brings healing and strengthens the relationship with the angels who guide us, helped by mandarin, chamomile and neroli.
Archangel Metatron	When we need to make a transition in our lives, or perhaps heal a broken heart, ask Metatron to help with rose otto, lavender and geranium.
Archangel Michael	When we feel we need protection or are fearful, the warrior Michael will come forward to help us. Use ginger, lime, vetiver and rosemary.
Archangel Jophiel	Boost your energy and self-confidence with Jophiel's support using ylang ylang, mandarin and bergamot.

The mathematician and mystic Pythagoras believed that numbers were spiritual and each had special significance. Over thousands of years, the interpretation of numbers has grown into the science of numerology and, according to this, the double number 11:11 is a 'master number' with an angelic connection. Many people say that this number seems to keep turning up frequently, more than any other, for example when they glance at the clock or look at their phone. This means that our spirit guides are trying to get our attention and when I see 11:11 I know there's a special message for me. Other doubled numbers also have their own meanings:

22:22   This is your angels asking you to keep faith. They are letting you know they are by your side.

33:33   The angels are reassuring you that your plans are going well and your prayers have been answered.

44:44   Don't give up! You need to continue to work hard at fulfilling your dreams and will succeed with angelic help.

55:55   Have patience and create harmony so that the desired improvements you are working on can be manifested.

66:66   It's a time to pay special attention to family life and abundance.

77:77   You have listened to the angels and are receiving the divine guidance you require.

88:88   You have the inner wisdom to manifest the angelic realm and the angels are helping you to achieve that.

99:99   Something in life is ending and the angels are showing you a new direction, working behind the scenes to help you find your calling.

10:10   It's a time for personal development and spiritual awaking so listen to your intuition and be prepared to step outside your comfort zone.

Angelology is the study of how astrological signs are linked to particular angels, helping us to have a better understanding of their presence in our lives.

Aries   Archangel Ariel is powerful just like Aries people, who have a strong work ethic and vitality. Call upon Ariel when planning new ventures.

Taurus   Archangel Chamuel is a peacemaker who communicates with people to avoid the emotional conflicts that Taureans sometimes find themselves involved in. Also connected by the love of nature and the finer things of life.

Gemini   Geminis are intellectual and emotionally charged, sharing the same kind of mathematical mind as Archangel Zadkiel, who loves problem-solving. He brings comfort to those in need too.

Cancer   Archangel Gabriel is guardian of the family, which Cancerians love. Financial security and sensitivity towards children are important characteristics that Gabriel supports.

Leo   Archangel Raziel's knowledge is total and perfect, marrying nicely with the intelligent and fiery Leos. With Raziel's help they also have great power to heal by giving love and laughter.

Virgo   Virgos are good at problem-solving and with the vibrant Archangel Metatron also have amazing healing energy. There is a connection here with Near-Death Experiences too.

Libra   Archangel Jophiel helps us see the beauty in life by making the right decisions, in harmony with the diplomatic Libran. They weigh up what people need and give support. Jophiel is a wonderful cleanser of negative energy.

Scorpio   Scorpios can be secretive and a bit spiky but Archangel Jeremiel helps to banish any negative energy. Working together, they can create hope for those in despair.

Sagittarius   Raguel is the archangel of reconciliation, forgiveness and new friendships, and Sagittarians likewise remain neutral in conflict. They team up to offer love and loyalty to others.

Capricorn   Capricorns have an understanding of the afterlife so it's not surprising that Azrael, the archangel of death, is connected with them. They make a tough combination, able to heal any heart with their love.

Aquarius   The brilliant Aquarians use their heads rather than their hearts, supported by the vitality and wisdom of Archangel Uriel, spreading peace and light to everyone.

Pisces   Pisceans and Archangel Sandalphon make wonderful music together, with the delicate and soft characteristics of the angelic realm.

The special energies of crystals also bring us closer to the angels and many of us feel a bond with a particular one, especially if it is linked to our astrological sign and worn or carried with us every day. I have always used crystals in my spiritual work; we know we're using the right one when it 'speaks' to us with heat or pins and needles in our fingers.

Crystals are often used for healing but they are important in every aspect of life, giving us confidence and helping us to solve problems. The ones associated with our zodiac signs can attract different angels to those described before, bringing new qualities to our relationship with them.

Aries   Chamuel is the archangel of pure love and happy relationships, his name appropriately means 'he who sees God'. The Apache tears crystal is a natural bringer of abundance and acts as a channel for spirit, shielding us from harm and attracting love.

Taurus Known as 'the grace of God', Hagiel (also known as Anael) invokes reliability and practicality along with red beryl, the crystal of warmth and support and a stone of passion. This crystal, held up to the light, can attract your soulmate with Hagiel's help.

Gemini Rainbow Moonstone is gentle and will offer healing and strength. It is associated with the Moon goddess Selina and with fertility. Use this and nurture yourself in the loving arms of the master healer Archangel Raphael.

Cancer Variscite offers contact with deceased relatives so is linked with Archangel Gabriel, who supports our souls on the way to Heaven. It is also as a fertility crystal and Gabriel is known as the angel of children and families.

Leo Ask the wise Archangel Michael to show you your spiritual pathway while holding blue jasper. Both crystal and angel offer protection and encourage you to speak truth without fear.

Virgo The wise woman of the celestial hierarchy is Archangel Jophiel who comes forward with spiritual knowledge, especially when you connect with gold-flecked lapis lazuli, the crystal of truth and friendship.

Libra Archangel Hagiel has the gentle traits of harmony and peaceful living. He is twinned with the beautiful, gentle celestite to bring spiritual knowledge.

Scorpio Tiger's eye brings empowerment to the user and the confidence to succeed, as well as protection from psychic harm. It is linked with the powerful Archangel Azrael.

Sagittarius	Morganite helps us to avoid arguments and conflict, opening channels of communication, supported by Archangel Raziel.
Capricorn	Archangel Asriel governs the seas and brings intuition, wisdom and dreams. The manifestation star quartz crystal is magical when linked with Asriel to manifest your heart's desire.
Aquarius	Amethyst chevron will help you build confidence in your own choices, known for its guidance properties particularly alongside Archangel Uriel, who brings flashes of inspiration.
Pisces	The archangel of mercy and benevolence, Zadkiel, helps to diffuse aggression and create peace. Reach out to him using jade during your meditation.

I hope you now know, if you didn't already, that the angels are always beside us, giving their love and support. So let's end this book by going back to the beginning, with one of my earliest experiences of angelic guidance that taught me we can call upon their help whenever we need it.

When I was around thirteen years-old, my Uncle Derek was learning how to drive taught by my Uncle Alan. Derek was rather fiery whilst Alan was a placid character. In our area the roads were quiet with not many cars about in those days, so one day I went with them because they were heading for Clumber Park in Nottinghamshire where there's the ancient Major Oak tree that is supposed to have sheltered Robin Hood and his men.

My uncles started arguing about which way to go and, when we did eventually arrive, Derek stormed off with Alan following and trying to calm him down. So I thought, as kids do, that I'd just go and find the Major Oak myself… Well, I wandered around for ages until, of course, I realised that I was completely lost in the cold, silent woods. I was very scared. Then my Grandma Mac's words came back to me: "Whenever you are in trouble, call upon the angels to help you", so I sat down on a fallen branch and prayed for help to get me back to the car.

After a minute or so, a pink light appeared in front of me and I knew I had to follow it as it moved along the paths, guiding me back to safety. My uncles were so relieved to find me that they stopped arguing. In fact, while we were driving home they were in such a good mood that they were singing at the tops of their voices and not really concentrating on the road. Suddenly, a very loud voice coming out of nowhere shouted, "Brake!", and Derek did a perfect emergency stop just as a fawn ran into the road in front of us, the mother deer watching on from the other side.

I was now convinced about angelic love and guidance. But I never did get to see the Major Oak.

If you have enjoyed this book...

Local Legend is committed to publishing the very best spiritual writing, both fiction and non-fiction. You might also enjoy:

GHOSTS OF THE NHS
Glynis Amy Allen (ISBN 978-1-910027-34-9)

It is rare to find an account of interaction with the spirit world that is so wonderfully down-to-earth! The author simply gives us one extraordinary true story after another, as entertaining as they are evidential. Glynis, an hereditary medium, worked for thirty years as a senior hospital nurse in the National Health Service, mostly in A&E wards. Almost on a daily basis, she would see patients' souls leave their bodies escorted by spirit relatives or find herself working alongside spirit doctors – not to mention the Grey Lady, a frequent ethereal visitor! A unique contribution to our understanding of life, this book was an immediate bestseller.

THE QUIRKY MEDIUM
Alison Wynne-Ryder (ISBN 978-1-907203-47-3)

Alison is the co-host of the TV show *Rescue Mediums*, in which she puts herself in real danger to free homes of lost and often malicious spirits. Yet she is a most reluctant medium, afraid of ghosts! This is her amazing and often very funny autobiography, taking us backstage of the television production as well as describing how she came to discover the psychic gifts that have brought her an international following.

Winner of the Silver Medal in the national
Wishing Shelf Book Awards.
"Almost impossible to put down."

DAY TRIPS TO HEAVEN

T J Hobbs (ISBN 978-1-907203-99-2)

The author's debut novel is a brilliant description of life in the spiritual worlds and of the guidance available to all of us on Earth as we struggle to be the best we can. Ethan is learning to be a spirit guide but having a hard time of it, with too many questions and too much self-doubt. But he has potential, so is given a special dispensation to bring a few deserving souls for a preview of the afterlife, to help them with crucial decisions they have to make in their lives. The book is full of gentle humour, compassion and spiritual knowledge, and it asks important questions of us all.

AURA CHILD

A I Kaymen (ISBN 978-1-907203-71-8)

One of the most astonishing books ever written, telling the true story of a genuine Indigo child. Genevieve grew up in a normal London family but from an early age realised that she had very special spiritual and psychic gifts. She saw the energy fields around living things, read people's thoughts and even found herself slipping through time and able to converse with the spirits of those who had lived in her neighbourhood. This is an uplifting and inspiring book for what it tells us about the nature of our minds.

SPIRIT SHOWS THE WAY

Pam Brittan (ISBN 978-1-910027-28-8)

A clairvoyant medium for over thirty years and highly respected throughout the UK, Pam describes herself as "an ordinary woman with an extraordinary gift." Despite many personal difficulties, she has shared this gift tirelessly and brought comfort and understanding of the Spirit to a great many people. Here, she inspires us to realise our own innate gifts and to trust that Spirit will always guide us on the right path.

CELESTIAL AMBULANCE

Ann Matkins (ISBN 978-1-907203-45-9)

A brave and delightful comedy novel. Having died of cancer, Ben wakes up in the afterlife looking forward to a good rest, only to find that everyone is expected to get a job! He becomes the driver of an ambulance (with a mind of her own), rescuing the spirits of others who have died suddenly and delivering them safely home. This book is as thought-provoking as it is entertaining.
"A fun novel packed full of wisdom."
The Wishing Shelf Book Awards.

TAP ONCE FOR YES

Jacquie Parton (ISBN 978-1-907203-62-6)

This extraordinary book offers powerful evidence of human survival after death. When Jacquie's son Andrew suddenly committed suicide, she was devastated. But she was determined to find out whether his spirit lived on, and began to receive incredible yet undeniable messages from him on her mobile phone... Several others also then described deliberate attempts at spirit contact. This is a story of astonishing love and courage, as Jacquie fought her own grief and others' doubts in order to prove to the world that her son still lives.
"A compelling read." *The national Wishing Shelf Book Awards.*

HAUNTED BY PAST LIVES

Sarah Truman (ISBN 978-1-910027-13-4)

When Sarah's partner told her that she had murdered him, she took little notice. After all, dreams don't mean anything, do they? But Tom's recurring and vividly detailed dreams demanded to be investigated and so the pair embarked upon thorough and professional historical research, uncovering previously unknown facts that seemed to lead to only one simple conclusion: past lives are true! Yet even that was not the end of their story, for they had unwittingly lifted the lid on some dramatic supernatural phenomena...

POWER FOR GOOD

David J Serlin (ISBN 978-1-910027-31-8)

When we say "Yes!" to the subtle invitations of Spirit, we may find ourselves on exciting journeys of discovery and learning, drawing to ourselves a universal Power for Good that changes us forever. David describes how a chance encounter – and an open mind – led to almost incredible psychic experiences and revelations of spiritual teachings that took him and his wife Linda on a whole new path and new careers. He tells their story here and sets out, in down-to-earth language and with humour, the principles for a happy and fulfilled life.

Local Legend titles are available as paperbacks and eBooks.
Further details and extracts of these and many other
beautiful books for the Mind, Body and Spirit
may be seen at

www.local-legend.co.uk

CPSIA information can be obtained
at www.ICGtesting.com
Printed in the USA
LVHW080434130421
684331LV00014B/433